How We Get Along

In *How We Get Along*, philosopher J. David Velleman compares our social interactions to the interactions among improvisational actors on stage. He argues that we play ourselves – not artificially but authentically, by doing what would make sense coming from us as we really are. And like improvisational actors, we deal with one another in dual capacities: both as characters within the social drama and as players contributing to the shared performance.

In this conception of social intercourse, Velleman finds rational grounds for morality, though not a rational guarantee. He maps a middle course between skepticism and rationalism, arguing that practical reasoning is "pro-moral" without requiring moral action. The result is what he calls a "kinda Kantian metaethics."

Written in an accessible and engaging style, *How We Get Along* is the summation of Velleman's thinking to date, incorporating and unifying previous work on agency, the self, the emotions, narrative, and Kantian moral theory.

J. David Velleman is Professor of Philosophy at New York University. He is the author of *Practical Reflection, The Possibility of Practical Reason*, and most recently, *Self to Self*. He is also a founding editor of the online journal *Philosophers' Imprint*.

How We Get Along

J. DAVID VELLEMAN

CAMBRIDGE
UNIVERSITY PRESS

0237048331

CAMBRIDGE UNIVERSITY PRESS
Cambridge, New York, Melbourne, Madrid, Cape Town, Singapore, São Paulo, Delhi

Cambridge University Press
32 Avenue of the Americas, New York, NY 10013–2473, USA

www.cambridge.org
Information on this title: www.cambridge.org/9780521043403

First published 2009

Printed in the United States of America

A catalog record for this publication is available from the British Library.

Library of Congress Cataloging in Publication data
Velleman, James David.
How we get along / J. David Velleman.
p.   cm.
Includes bibliographical references (p.   ) and index.
ISBN 978-0-521-88853-0 (hardback) – ISBN 978-0-521-04340-3 (pbk.)
1. Practical reason.   2. Ethics.   3. Acting.   4. Improvisation (Acting)   I. Title.
BC177. V45 2009
128'.4–dc22   2008031158

ISBN 978-0-521-88853-0 hardback
ISBN 978-0-521-04340-3 paperback

For Daniel and Evan

Contents

Preface ix

Introduction 1

1 Acting 9

2 Reacting 35

3 Interacting 59

4 Reflecting 89

5 Foundations 115

6 Theory 159

7 Meaning 185

Bibliography 207

Index 215

Preface

I began this project in preparation for the Shearman Lectures, which I was invited to deliver at University College, London, in May 2007. Those three lectures – revised, expanded, and sub-divided – appear here as Lectures 1, 2, 3, and 5.[1] I am grateful

[1] Before they were delivered, those lectures were discussed with the members of a seminar led by Michael Smith at Princeton University in the fall of 2006, and with the members of a seminar led by Christine Korsgaard at Harvard University in the winter of 2007. A paper covering the material in Lectures 1 and 2 was delivered to a one-day conference at York University organized by Christian Piller (May 2007) and to the British Society for Ethical Theory (July 2007). That version appeared in *Ethics* 18 (2008) under the title "A Theory of Value." Portions of Lectures 1 and 2 were contained in a paper entitled "Love and Non-Existence," which was presented to the graduate student colloquium at New York University (February 2008); to The Fourth Steven Humphrey Excellence in Philosophy Conference at the University of California, Santa Barbara (February 2008), where the commentator was Mark Schroeder; and to a conference at Northwestern University (March 2008). It appeared in *Philosophy and Public Affairs* as Part 3 of an article entitled "Persons in Prospect."

Originally, the first lecture in this series consisted of what are now parts of Lectures 1 through 3. Under the title "Action as Improv," that lecture was discussed by the philosophy reading group at Boston University (January 2007) and by a workshop on trust organized at Yale by Matthew Noah Smith and Adrienne Martin (April 2007). It was presented to a conference on agency organized by Christian Miller at Wake Forest University

to the Philosophy Department of UCL and especially its chair, Jo Wolff, for the honor of giving the Shearman Lectures and for three days of wonderful discussion and hospitality in London.

Having written three lectures, I found myself with more to say and an inclination to say it in the same voice, as if presenting additional lectures. In reality, Lectures 4, 6, and 7 have never been presented. Casting myself in a role even larger than that of Shearman lecturer is presumptuous indeed; I hope that it will prove to have benefited the reader, by encouraging me to express myself more briefly and informally than usual.

Beyond their overt topic, these lectures pursue a private agenda of mine, which is to locate the intersection of various themes that I have hitherto pursued independently, with only the vague hope that they would some day intersect.² One theme is an analysis of practical reasoning as a process of making sense

in September 2006; as the Parcells Lecture at the University of Connecticut in October 2006; as the Lipkind Lecture at the University of Chicago in April 2007; and to a conference on Selfhood, Normativity and Control organized by Jan Bransen in Nijmegen (May 2007), where the commentator was Maureen Sie. The lecture was also presented to the Philosophy Departments of the University of Southern California (January 2007), the University of Richmond (March 2007), and Davidson College (March 2007).

  Lecture 5 was discussed at a workshop in the Philosophy Department of the University of Chicago (April 2007); at a meeting of the Mid-Atlantic Reading Group in Ethics (September 2007); and at the NYU Philosophy Department's Mind and Language Seminar (January 2008), where Paul Boghossian presented a valuable summary and critique. Parts of the lecture were also presented to the Philosophy Department at Cornell University (September 2008).

² The gaps between these themes were insightfully pointed out by Catriona Mackenzie in a paper titled "Bare Personhood? Velleman on Selfhood," which was presented to a conference on my book *Self to Self*, organized by Jeannette Kennett and Steve Matthews in May 2006 at the Centre for Applied Philosophy and Public Ethics, the Australian National University. Mackenzie's paper was published in *Philosophical Explorations* 10 (2007): 263–81.

of oneself in causal-psychological terms. Another theme is an analysis of narrative as conveying a mode of understanding – and, specifically, self-understanding – that is distinct from the understanding conveyed by causal explanation. A third theme is an interpretation of Kant's conception of practical law in terms of common knowledge among rational agents. A final theme is the nature of the moral emotions of love, shame, and guilt. All of these themes were sounded in my book *Self to Self: Selected Essays*,[3] although the second remained largely undeveloped until a subsequent paper, which here supplies the central sections of Lecture 7.[4]

In tying these themes together, I reprise arguments that are spelled out at greater length in my first book, *Practical Reflection*,[5] or as well as *Self to Self* and an earlier collection of papers, *The Possibility of Practical Reason*.[6] Lecture 5 supersedes the Introduction to *The Possibility of Practical Reason*, which made claims that I now regard as mistaken.

I am grateful to many friends and colleagues who have read and commented on the manuscript of these lectures, including: Paul Boghossian, David Copp, Stephen Darwall, Andy Egan, David Enoch, Melis Erdur, Herlinde Pauer-Studer, David Plunkett, Nishi Shah, Matthew Silverstein, Sharon Street, and Helena Wright. I am especially grateful to Jeff Sebo for a close reading and critique of the penultimate draft. Thanks also to Beatrice Rehl, my editor at Cambridge, and to my manuscript editor, Russell Hahn.

---

3 New York: Cambridge University Press, 2006.
4 "Narrative Explanation," *Philosophical Review* 112 (2003): 1–25.
5 Princeton, NJ: Princeton University Press, 1988; reprinted in 2007 by the CSLI Press.
6 *The Possibility of Practical Reason* (Oxford: Oxford University Press, 2000). This book, now out of print, is available on my personal home page, http://homepages.nyu.edu/~dv26/.

Introduction

Amongst its many other infirmities, most analytical moral philosophy proceeds without ever clearly focusing on the social as a determining feature of individual action and motivation.

Simon Blackburn[1]

Maybe the grounding of morality lies closer to the social surface than philosophers like to think, neither in the structure of practical reason nor in a *telos* of human nature but rather in our mundane ways of muddling through together – that is, in how we get along. Our ways of getting along must themselves rest on the bedrock of practical reason and human nature, but they may form, as it were, a layer of topsoil without which morality could never take root. If so, then asking how moral norms can sprout straight out of our rationality or humanity may be futile.

---

[1] *Ruling Passions* (Oxford: Clarendon Press, 1998), 30–1. In quoting Blackburn on the failure of analytic moral philosophy to focus on "the social," I should also note that there are significant exceptions, including: Elizabeth Anderson, *Value in Ethics and Economics* (Cambridge, MA: Harvard University Press, 1993); Joseph Raz, *The Practice of Value*, ed. R. Jay Wallace (Oxford: Clarendon Press, 2003); Barbara Herman, *Moral Literacy* (Cambridge, MA: Harvard University Press, 2007); and Tamar Schapiro, "Compliance, Complicity, and the Nature of Nonideal Conditions," *Journal of Philosophy* 100 (2003): 329–55.

This image suggests that moral philosophers ought to take a closer look at the social surface of our dealings together as autonomous human beings. In the lectures that follow, I pursue this suggestion by considering how our mundane interactions are informed by our recognition of one another's agency. How does that mutual recognition shape our collective life?

My answer to this question will ultimately lead to a metaethics that is in some respects rationalist and in others skeptical.[2] My metaethics is rationalist in that it grounds morality in social phenomena that are themselves supported by practical reasoning. But morality is thus supported by rationality at one remove; and so its underpinnings are less secure than is generally claimed in rationalist metaethics. In my view, practical reason is not in itself moral; it is merely pro-moral, in that it has encouraged us to develop a moral way of life. There was no antecedent guarantee that such a way of life would develop among rational agents, much less that moral conduct will be rationally required of every agent at all times. The most that metaethics can do in this regard is to show how the moral aspects of our way of life can be seen retrospectively as a rational development, a form of progress.

Showing that practical reasoning is pro-moral thus leaves room for skepticism. This skepticism is not a matter of doubting whether we have "reason to be moral"; it is rather a matter of appreciating the contingency of morality, the possibility of its having failed to develop, and indeed the possibility of social or individual configurations from which various kinds of rational progress, including morality, are not rationally accessible. Perhaps a better term for this attitude than 'skepticism' would be 'insecurity'. From my insecure perspective, Kant's assurance that all rational agents have "the moral law within" sounds naively complacent.

---

[2] My skepticism bears many similarities to the views expressed by Bernard Williams in *Ethics and the Limits of Philosophy* (Cambridge, MA: Harvard University Press, 1985).

I am also skeptical about the reach of moral philosophy. I think of practical reasoning as an experimental discipline. At the social level where morality originates, practical reasoning involves the sort of muddling through together that I describe as "getting along." Where this process will lead is as unpredictable as the outcome of scientific inquiry – which is why philosophy can provide no more than a *post facto* commentary on where it has led thus far. Moral philosophy speaks to morality, in my view, as the philosophy of science speaks to science – that is, as a methodological commentator and critic rather than as a substantive contributor.[3]

My other metaethical claims must be read in light of my skepticism about the reach of moral philosophy. When I argue that practical reasoning as I conceive it is pro-moral, I can easily be misinterpreted as trying to give an a priori guarantee that morality will turn out to be rational according to my view. But according to my view, a priori guarantees are not to be had in the practical realm any more than in the empirical.

There is an even deeper level at which I am skeptical about morality: I doubt whether it exists in the form traditionally envisioned by philosophers. In my view, there is no unitary point of view, source of reasons, or deliberative principle to which the term 'morality' refers. Morality as I describe it is distributed holographically throughout our way of life, in the form of various attitudes and practices that are united only by family resemblances, which show forth only in a particular light. Among the reasons why I don't consider whether we have "reason to be moral," then, is that I don't think that "moral" describes any one way of being. I therefore offer no theory of moral reasons, no analysis of the moral 'ought', no metaphysics of moral facts or properties.

[3] This view is described and rejected by John McDowell in "Virtue and Reason," in *Mind, Value, and Reality* (Cambridge, MA: Harvard University Press, 1998), 50–73, p. 50. See also Philip Pettit, "Substantive Moral Theory," *Social Philosophy and Policy* 25 (2008): 1–27.

In this respect, my metaethics may strike some philosophers as no metaethics at all. I will happily cede the term to these philosophers, though I don't know what term to adopt in its place.

Finally, my view is skeptical about practical reason itself, in two respects. First, I demote practical reason from the conductor's podium on which it is traditionally pictured, leading the performance. I picture practical reason less as an orchestral conductor than as a theatrical prompter – out of sight, following the action in case it needs to be nudged back onto an intelligible course.

Secondly, my view postulates a discontinuity in the structure of practical reasoning. Practical reasoning aims for overall coherence in ourselves, our reactions, and our actions, but there are at least two modes of coherence at which it can aim, in my view: explanatory coherence and narrative coherence. These modes of coherence can themselves be made to cohere with one another, but they can also pull us in opposite directions. Here again, my rationalism gives no guarantees.

Among the few and tentative practical implications that can be derived from my brand of metaethics, some have surprised even me, and not always pleasantly. For example, I find myself committed to taking a more conservative attitude toward conventional morality than I am accustomed to take. I'd like to think that my willingness to entertain this attitude is a sign of intellectual honesty. It may just be a sign of age.

✳ ✳ ✳

The key argument of these lectures can be put like this.

In order to lie to someone, we must first share a language with him. And whereas self-interested reasoning may counsel each of us to defect from the cooperative practice of truth telling, which therefore has the incentive structure of a prisoner's dilemma, language has the incentive structure of a coordination problem, in which self-interested reasoning counsels each of us to converge with others rather than make an exception for himself. Even when self-interest opposes telling the truth to others, it still favors speaking their language.

In these lectures, I argue that the prisoner's dilemmas in which individual practical reasoning seems to favor antisocial behavior rest atop the solution to a coordination problem, in the same way as the incentives to lying rest atop a shared language. The underlying language in the former case – the language of behavior – is a vocabulary of action-types and practices, which individual practical reasoning counsels us to share with others, so that we can understand our dealings with them.

Now, imagine that we could develop a spoken language that somehow contained incentives against lying, or at least against putting oneself in the way of temptations to lie. Our individual interests would favor converging on such a language, since each would gain more from its deterrent effect on others than he would lose from the like effect on himself, and those gains and losses would be inseparable, given the shared need for linguistic convergence. The underlying coordination problem of language would therefore reach a solution that afforded no basis – or, at least, a much narrower basis – for a prisoner's dilemma that threatens the practice of truth telling.

This outcome is of course an idle fantasy, since languages don't contain intrinsic incentives (except for the very weak incentives of emotionally colored words such as "liar"). But I shall argue that a vocabulary of action-types and practices contains significant incentives, because it structures our practical reasoning, by framing the options over which we deliberate. The shared practical vocabulary that we develop can include incentives that minimize, or enable us to circumvent or solve, the prisoner's dilemmas that we face when acting within that vocabulary. Each of us has an interest in converging with the others on such a practical vocabulary. And morality comprises a family of trends and patterns in the way of life on which we consequently converge.

Traditionally, moral philosophy has attempted to imagine how human beings could work their way out of a state of nature into a state of sociality. But most moral philosophy conjures up an impure, less-than-natural state of nature, in which the practical options are already framed. In the terms of my linguistic analogy, the inhabitants are imagined as trying to develop a cooperative scheme of truth telling in a language that they already share. In my view, however, the work of developing the cooperative scheme must begin at the stage of developing a language that will be hospitable to it. When moral philosophers begin their thought experiment with a population that already shares a vocabulary, they have skipped the stage at which the foundations of morality are laid.

＊　＊　＊

The lectures proceed in the following order.

Lecture 1 introduces my conception of practical reasoning. This conception is one that I have presented many times before, but it is here recast in terms that are more readily applicable to social relations among rational agents.

Lecture 2 expands my conception of practical reasoning to include reasoning about how to feel as well as how to act.

Lecture 3 applies my conception of practical reasoning to social interaction. It asks: How are relations among people informed by their recognition of one another as practical reasoners in my sense of the term?

Lecture 4 explains why practical reasoners, as I conceive them, might have a psychological mechanism roughly corresponding to our commonsense notion of a conscience.

Lecture 5 explains how my conception of agency bears on the foundations of ethics. It is primarily about metaethics – or, rather, about what is left of metaethics under my skeptical view.

Lecture 6 explores what is left of normative theory under a view like mine, which regards the normative as largely an empirical matter. The lecture asks: if moral philosophy can accomplish as little as I suggested in Lecture 5, why do we bother with abstract theories of right and wrong?

Lecture 7 explains the difference between psychological self-understanding and the self-understanding derived from story-telling. This difference yields two distinct and not necessarily coordinated trends in practical reasoning

1

Acting

My eventual topic will be what we philosophers call morality. In speaking of the moral as a distinct realm of thought and discourse, we trust that others will know what we mean, but in my experience, many people unschooled in philosophy have no idea. The reason, I suspect, is that what we call morality is no more than a family of patterns running through our way of life, held together by no more than family resemblances that only some people have been trained to recognize.

I want to explain how these moral patterns emerge from our nature as rational agents. I am going to argue that rational agency does not mandate these patterns, much less the individual actions of which they consist, but that it does induce them in our way of life, through a gradual and contingent process of collective practical reasoning. Before getting to that argument, however, I need to explain how rational agency works, and how it might give rise to something like morality, if not directly to morality itself.

When I eventually get to talk about morality, I won't have a lot to say about it. The main thing I have to say will be that there is not a lot for philosophers to say about morality – in any case, not as much as many philosophers have tried to say. I hope to make up the deficit by talking about many related things, starting now with action.

When I speak of action, I mean something more than mere bodily movement.[1] The difference can be cast into relief by a comparison between actions and non-actions involving the same overt behavior. Consider the behavior of crying.[2]

Crying can be a completely involuntary outpouring of emotion, as when a person bursts into tears at the first shock of pain, disappointment, or grief. At the opposite extreme, crying can be entirely contrived, as when a six-year-old prolongs his wails long after his pain or disappointment has obviously passed, until we chide him for "faking it." Between these extremes lies the authentic but also voluntary behavior of the adult who, after absorbing the first shock, indulges in a good cry. This person is

---

[1] I agree with Harry Frankfurt that the concept of human action may be "a special case of another concept whose range is much wider," in that it encompasses action on the part of nonhuman organisms ("The Problem of Action," *American Philosophical Quarterly* 15 [1978]: 157–62; reprinted in *The Importance of What We Care About* [Cambridge: Cambridge University Press, 1988], 69–79, p. 79). As Frankfurt explains, the generic concept is that of behavior controlled by the organism, not just by one of its constituent subsystems or parts. Of course, behavior may be controlled by the organism in virtue of being controlled by a particular, privileged subsystem or part, which is authorized, as it were, to control behavior on the organism's behalf. On that premise – which I accept – a theory of human action must explain which subsystem or part of the human organism is privileged in this way, and why it is so privileged. I do not offer the latter explanation in these lectures. See instead "What Happens When Someone Acts?," *Mind* 101 (1992): 461–81, reprinted in *The Possibility of Practical Reason* (Oxford: Oxford University Press, 2000), 123–43; and "Identification and Identity," in *The Contours of Agency: Essays on Themes from Harry Frankfurt*, ed. Sarah Buss and Lee Overton (Cambridge, MA: MIT Press, 2001), 91–123, reprinted in *Self to Self* (New York: Cambridge University Press, 2006), 330–60. See also "The Way of the Wanton," in *Practical Identity and Narrative Agency*, ed. Kim Atkins and Catriona MacKenzie (London: Routledge, 2007), 169–92.

[2] Everything I will say about crying could be said *mutatis mutandis* about laughing as well. Both are reflex behaviors that can be taken up, to a greater or lesser extent, into voluntary actions.

not faking it: he[3] is sincerely expressing real emotion. But crying is in his case an action rather than a fit of passion. His behavior is still propelled by emotion, but it is also shaped by him into an act of crying. In this respect, I believe, it can serve as a model of agency.

To begin with, this person is letting himself cry. He doesn't just let himself go, however, exerting no control over his behavior: he allows himself to cry but not to bellow or to fall on the floor or to tear at his clothes. Or maybe he does tear at his clothes a bit, if doing so is part of his conception of crying. After all, people have different ways of crying, even if it is at bottom a physiologically programmed behavior common to all human beings. Some rend their garments, some sniffle into tissues, some shout out lamentations. And these differences aren't merely idiosyncratic: they are culturally conditioned, reflecting different conventions for the expression of sad emotion. "Having a cry" means different things in different times and places.

Differences in how people cry might be attributed to ingrained habits that embody each person's knowledge of how to cry. But surely there are adults who cry only once in ten or twenty years, and they are not remembering how to cry by calling up habits acquired in childhood. A more plausible explanation is that different people have different conceptions of crying. A person who actively cries does not just let some behavioral program take over: he has an idea of what he's doing, and he brings the manifestations of his emotion into accord with that idea. His emotion initially propelled him blindly, but now it carries him through the witting fulfillment of an action-concept that he has in mind.

* * *

The agent now resembles a "method" actor – that is, an actor who employs the method taught by Lee Strasberg in the Actor's Studio.

---

[3] I use 'he' as the unmarked pronoun, which is semantically gender-neutral.

The method actor portrays motives, thoughts, and feelings by actually having and manifesting them, while also modulating their manifestations to fit the part that he is playing. He doesn't simulate the manifestations of grief; he musters the emotion itself; but then he doesn't just let his grief manifest itself, since he needs to manifest it in character. So he channels the outpourings of his emotion into his conception of how the character would behave, relying on the emotion to carry him through his enactment of the role.

Of course, the crying of a theatrical actor involves considerable duplicity, even if the actor is using "the method" and hence really feeling the relevant emotion. His acting still involves duplicity, first, because he has deliberately summoned up his emotion with the help of thoughts about matters unrelated to the drama (such as the thoughts that Strasberg called "sense memory");[4] and, second, because the emotion and its manifestations have been dictated to him by a script. According to the fiction of the drama, the actor's character is responding to his circumstances with spontaneous behavior that expresses a spontaneous emotion. In this respect, what the fictional character is doing, the actor is merely pretending to do.

Even this contrast will not apply if the actor is participating in improvisational theater, where the action is unscripted. There the fiction of a character behaving spontaneously is itself enacted spontaneously by the actor, and so the gap between fiction and reality is narrowed. Consider, then, how improvisational acting must work.[5]

---

[4] See Lee Strasberg, *A Dream of Passion: The Development of the Method* (New York: Plume, 1988). Strasberg used the term 'sense memory' for the technique of vividly recalling the sensory qualities of an experience that once aroused the emotion to be portrayed.

[5] For an extended inquiry into the analogy between everyday action and improvisational theater, see R. Keith Sawyer, *Creating Conversations:*

An improvisational actor must first of all understand his character and the character's circumstances. He must have an idea of how his character is motivated under those circumstances – how the circumstances engage the character's wants, values, convictions, habits, emotions, and traits of personality, thereby making it intelligible for him to behave. And he must then enact an idea of how the character *would* behave – "would" in the sense that the behavior makes sense coming from that character in those circumstances. The relevant notion of "making sense" is not normative: it's not about what the character ought to do. It's the notion of what can be understood in terms of the character's attributes and attitudes under the circumstances. The understanding that must be possible, if an action is to make sense coming from the character, is a folk-psychological understanding that traces the action to its causes in the motives, traits, and other dispositions of the character. If the actor's behavior cannot be attributed to causes within the character in this sense, then it will not be "in character,"[6] and

Improvisation in Everyday Discourse (Cresskill, NJ: Hampton Press, 2001); *Pretend Play as Improvisation: Conversation in the Preschool Classroom* (Mahwah, NJ: Lawrence Erlbaum Associates, 1997). See also Erving Goffman, *The Presentation of Self in Everyday Life* (New York: Anchor Books, 1959).

[6] The phrase "in character" is potentially misleading in some contexts. In the character-based arts, such as theater, film, and cinematic animation, creating a believable character requires endowing him with a relatively small set of clearly recognizable characteristics. Though such a characterization is necessary in order to make a fictional figure believable, it is actually unrealistic; for if it were applied to a real person, it would be so simplistic as to be a caricature.

I think that when we speak of a real person as acting "in character" or "out of character," we are in fact comparing his behavior to just such a simplistic stereotype, representing a few of his most marked characteristics. We mean that he is acting "to type" or "against type." But in the discussion that follows, I will use the term 'character' to denote, in the first instance, a person's self-concept, which is far more complex and subtle than a stereotype. I think of the self-concept as including a representation of his standing traits,

so the audience won't attribute it to the fictional character he is portraying; they will attribute it instead to the actor, as bad acting, or even as a departure from acting altogether, an interruption of the performance.

Other differences between actor and character remain. The actor knows that he is not actually in the situation fictionally confronting his character; he is personally unlike the character in many respects; and if he is to have any of the occurrent thoughts and feelings manifested by his character, he may have to induce them in himself by artificial means.

✳ ✳ ✳

I now ask you to join me in imagining away these remaining differences between an improvisational actor and the character he portrays. Imagine an actor who plays himself, responding to his actual circumstances and manifesting the occurrent thoughts and feelings that the circumstances actually arouse in him, given his actual attitudes and traits.

This actor improvises just as he did when portraying a fictional character, by enacting his idea of how it would be understandable for his character to manifest his thoughts and feelings under the circumstances. But now the character is himself, and so what would be understandable coming from the character, given the character's motives, is what would be understandable coming from him, given the motives he actually has. Thus, he manifests his actual thoughts and feelings, as elicited from his actual makeup by his actual circumstances, in accordance with his idea of what it makes sense for him to do in light of them.

Because this improviser will seek to enact the dispositions he has, and hence will generally have the dispositions he seeks to

his personal history, and the occurrent thoughts and feelings that he has at the present time. In my sense of the phrase, then, "acting in character" will mean, not "acting to type," but rather acting in accordance with everything that the agent knows or thinks about himself.

enact, he will tend to have two sources of motivation for whatever he does – the first-order dispositions that belong to him as the character, and the higher-order motive to make sense by enacting them, which belongs to him as the improvisational player. When there are conflicts among the former, first-order dispositions, the latter motive will tend to determine which one prevails, by adding its force to the one that strikes him as making most sense for his character to manifest.[7] He will then act partly out of the improviser's aim of giving the most plausible rendition of his character but also, like a method actor, out of the character's underlying motives, which will fund the enactment.

Now imagine that the improviser is terribly sad and disposed to cry. Maybe he starts to cry involuntarily, in an uncontrolled outpouring of emotion. If he doesn't already know that he is sad, and why he is sad, then crying won't fit his conception of the character he is playing, and so it will strike him as an unlikely thing for the character to do. He will therefore try to stop crying, so as not to spoil his rendition of the character. But if he knows what he is crying about, then crying may strike him as the very thing that his character would do under the circumstances, and so it will strike him as the very thing to enact, drawing on the tears supplied by his emotion. He will therefore cry out of genuine sadness but also under the guidance of his conception of crying as what it would make sense for his character to do.

In principle, the player could enact the idea of uncontrollable crying, but his character's sadness is not so great as to defy control; witness the fact that his crying is now under control, in virtue of being guided by his conception of it as making sense. Uncontrollable crying would not be in character, then, and so it isn't the thing for the player to enact. What would make sense

---

[7] If he misunderstands himself, he may try to enact a disposition he doesn't have – in which case he may fail to carry it off, thereby suffering *akrasia*, or weakness of will. Alternatively, he may find himself manifesting dispositions that he isn't trying to enact, with the result that his behavior is impulsive and perhaps even involuntary.

coming from the character is simply this: crying out of sadness
but also under the guidance of his conception of crying as what
would make sense. So that is what the player should enact –
whereupon, he will have fully merged with his character.[8]

✳ ✳ ✳

This result should have been obvious, I suppose: if a player is
going to play himself, then the role he plays had better be that
of a player playing himself. But what, you may ask, do these gambits of self-portrayal have to do with rational agency? An ordinary agent, minding his own business, is not standing before an
audience to whom he must give a plausible rendition of a character, not even of the character consisting in himself.[9] How could
the exigencies of character portrayal come to bear on him, in
his private capacity as a rational agent?

---

[8] In relying on the agent's self-conception, my account resembles Christine
Korsgaard's theory of "practical identities" (*The Sources of Normativity*
[Cambridge: Cambridge University Press, 1996]). There is one important difference. For Korsgaard, a practical identity is an evaluative self-conception –
"a description under which you find your life to be worth living and your
actions to be worth undertaking" (p. 101). The self-conception that figures
in my account of agency is not evaluative: it is a description under which your
actions and reactions make sense to you in causal-explanatory terms.

    Why do I prefer an account that relies on a nonevaluative self-concep-
tion? One reason is that I am hoping to explain values and valuing, and so I
need to avoid presupposing them. Another reason is that I want an account
of what is inescapable in agency, both conceptually, as a condition of being
an agent, and naturally, as an element of human nature. Trying to understand yourself is inescapable; finding your life worth living and your actions
worth undertaking is not. (The role of inescapability in my view is explored
further in Lecture 5.)

[9] Of course, this concession goes too far. When interacting with others, an
ordinary agent is indeed standing before an audience to whom he must
give a plausible rendition of himself. Social interactions will be the topic of
Lecture 3.

My answer is that the rational agent does have an audience, even if he is minding his own business – especially if he is minding his own business, in fact, since it is he who thereby serves as his own audience.[10] The agent is placed in this relation to himself by the combination of two distinctively human endowments: theoretical reason and objective self-awareness.

In theoretical reasoning, the human intellect functions not as a passive receptacle for information but as an active consumer. Anyone who has dealt at close quarters with infants or toddlers knows that the human animal is born with a voracious cognitive appetite.

During its second year, the child acquires a conception of itself as a cognizable object, a thing to be understood. And then it comes to see that understanding this particular thing is quite different from understanding any of the others. Other things must be understood as they are, however they may be.[11] But the cognizable object consisting in the inquirer himself is more cooperative, since it is disposed to instantiate what the inquirer *already* understands: it is so disposed because it consists in the inquirer himself, with his drive toward self-understanding. The inquirer learns that he can make sense *of* himself by making sense *to* himself – that is, by doing what makes sense to him.

---

[10] I discuss this point further in "The Centered Self," in *Self to Self* (New York: Cambridge University Press, 2006), 253–83. Goffman suggests that being his own audience commits the agent to inauthenticity: "Self-deception can be seen as something that results when two different roles, performer and audience, come to be compressed into the same individual" (*The Presentation of Self*, p. 81, n. 6; see also Goffman's concluding remarks on pp. 248–55). I disagree. The agent can play a role for his own observation without self-deception, provided that the role he performs is one of a self-observing performer.

[11] Of course, this statement doesn't apply to those "other things" which are of our own making – that is, to artifacts. But such things are the products of our actions, and to that extent they aren't "other" in the sense that I have in mind.

Once equipped with an objective self-concept, in other words, the naturally inquisitive human animal becomes an audience seeking to understand his own behavior, and he begins to accommodate this audience by enacting ideas of what it would be intelligible for him to do. He thus becomes the self-enacting improviser whom I have just described.[12]

I believe that the process of improvisational self-enactment consti- tutes practical reasoning, the process of choosing an action on the basis of reasons. Why do I think that the self-enactor chooses his action? Because it is his idea, which he puts into action in preference to other ideas that he might have enacted, if this one hadn't made more sense. Why do I think that he chooses for reasons? Because he chooses his action in light of a *rationale* for it, which consists in considerations in light of which the action makes sense.

When I say that this process constitutes practical reasoning, I am saying something different from what other philosophers are likely to hear. In association with that label, philosophers typically picture a list of considerations for and against alter- native courses of action, expressing thoughts that successively occupy an agent's attention up to the time at which he acts. I regard that picture as misguided, for several reasons.

It is true that if an agent is asked to justify his choice from among the alternatives, he can usually cite a few discrete

---

[12] See Alasdair MacIntyre, "The Intelligibility of Action," in *Rationality, Relativism and the Human Sciences*, ed. J. Margolis, M. Krausz, and R. M. Burian (Dordrecht: Martinus Nijhoff, 1986), 63–80, p. 64: "Intelligibility is ... not only a property which our actions must possess if they are to be understood by others as actions, to which response may then be made by further actions on their part. We ourselves have to be able to understand our own actions as intelligible ... if we are to be able to acknowledge them as actions rather than as something which we simply find ourselves doing, being as puzzled as anyone else as to what we are up to in doing whatever it is."

considerations in its favor. What he is citing, however, are features of his situation or himself that are especially relevant to understanding his action; or he may simply be directing the questioner's gaze to an angle from which self, situation, and action fall together into a comprehensible *Gestalt*. Sometimes the stated pros and cons were individuated and weighed in prior deliberation, but very rarely; they have usually been abstracted after the fact from what was a holistic process of entertaining possible conceptions of situation, self, and action, and then instantiating the one that best hangs together as an intelligible whole.

Philosophers who picture practical reasoning as a process of toting up pros and cons generally omit one important feature from their picture and overlook the presence of another. What's missing from their picture is a method for individuating favorable or unfavorable considerations and weighing how favorable or unfavorable they are.[13] I am proposing something like such a method, but without the assumption that considerations must be separated from one another in order to be weighed. Considerations weigh in favor of an action, I propose, insofar as they contribute to an overall understanding of the action, given how the agent conceives of himself and his situation. Individuating and weighing them separately is unnecessary, even counterproductive, since their contribution to the agent's overall self-understanding depends on its holistic features.

What's presupposed but generally overlooked in the standard picture of practical reasoning is the agent's self-awareness – his

---

[13] The mathematical model of decision theory sets limits of consistency on the weights attaching to those considerations, but within those very loose constraints, many different distributions of weight are possible, and the traditional picture includes no plausible method for determining which of the consistent distributions is correct. I discuss formal decision theory in "The Story of Rational Action," *Philosophical Topics* 21 (1993): 229–53, reprinted in *The Possibility of Practical Reason*, 144–69. On the definition of reasons as "considerations that count in favor," see Lecture 5, note 8.

implicit, unarticulated consciousness of the explicit thoughts
that he is traditionally pictured as articulating on his way to
choosing an action. His awareness of those thoughts is not
made explicit in the series of statements by which the thoughts
themselves are represented, and so it eludes philosophical consideration. When the agent's awareness of his thoughts is left
out of consideration, however, so is the rational structure of his
thinking.

✳ ✳ ✳

Let me illustrate this point with a series of thoughts that actually
occurred in the recent history of our discipline. Here is Bernard
Williams in Chapter 1 of his *Ethics and the Limits of Philosophy*:[14]

> Some philosophers have supposed that we cannot start from this
> general or indeterminate kind of practical question because
> questions such as "what should I do?", "what is the best way for me
> to live?", and so on, are *ambiguous* and sustain both a moral and
> a nonmoral sense. On this view, the first thing one would have to
> do with the question is to decide which of these different kinds of
> thing it meant, and until then one could not even start to answer
> it. That is a mistake. The analysis of meanings does not require
> "moral" and "nonmoral" as categories of meaning. Of course, if
> someone says of another "he is a good man," we can ask whether
> the speaker means that he is morally good, as contrasted, for
> instance, with meaning that he is a good man to take on a mili-
> tary sortie – but the fact that one can give these various interpre-
> tations no more yields a moral sense of "good" or of "good man"
> than it does a military sense (or a football sense, etc.).

Now, we can view these sentences as representing thoughts
that Williams framed "in his head" before writing them down;
or we can view them as thoughts that he framed directly on the
page – thinking aloud, as it were, but in writing. What I want to
point out about these sentences is that the rational connections

---

[14] Cambridge, MA: Harvard University Press, 1985, pp. 5–6.

holding them together are not logical connections between their propositional contents. In order to understand how these sentences hang together, you must understand that the first introduces an hypothesis, the second elaborates on it, the third rejects it, the fourth elaborates on that rejection, and the fifth begins by qualifying the elaboration and ends by restating it more precisely. What makes the paragraph intelligible is that it represents a process of thought that can be understood psychologically: hypothesis, elaboration, rejection; elaboration, qualification, restatement. Philosophical prose is argumentative primarily in this psychological sense; the notion that it consists primarily of logical arguments is a disciplinary myth, which I am tempted to call the Logical Fallacy.

I assume that Williams did not just spill these thoughts onto the page and find that they had followed an intelligible sequence; I rather assume that he composed them so as to be intelligibly sequential. What made them intelligibly sequential, though, was their psychological form, which was not articulated by the statements expressing the thoughts themselves but would have been articulated only by different statements, attributing the thoughts to their thinker. The form of Williams's thoughts would have been made explicit, in other words, only by the statements "I introduce an hypothesis, then I elaborate on it, then I reject it … ," and so forth. Williams didn't articulate those self-attributions, either in his head or in writing, but he did have the self-awareness whose contents they express. And the form in virtue of which his thoughts were intelligibly sequential was the form of those tacit self-attributions, which describe a psychologically intelligible sequence of thoughts. What held Williams's thoughts together, then, were connections that ran, not directly between the explicit contents of those thoughts, but indirectly, via the tacit self-attributions that constituted Williams's consciousness of thinking them.

*　*　*

So it is, I believe, with the thoughts that lead to action. If we ignore the agent's awareness of those thoughts, we will not be able to see what connects them to his action, just as we would miss the connections that held Williams's thoughts together if we considered only their explicit contents.

In the thoughts that are taken to embody an agent's practical reasoning, he is usually supplying himself with the materials for self-understanding, by thinking consciously about matters that interest him. He gathers materials for understanding possible courses of action by reacting to external circumstances in consciously valenced thoughts – thoughts that are consciously desirous or worried or fearful or joyous, as occasioned by the circumstances. Thoughts that are consciously desirous or fearful may illuminate intelligible lines of conduct better than further thoughts explicitly adverting to the agent's desire or fear, since the latter would be indicative of less-than-wholehearted desire or fear precisely because of their introspective focus.

In rare cases, an agent may consciously enumerate the pros and cons of various actions, as a way of disclosing to himself how he is inclined toward them. The agent has no metric for adding up or comparing these pros and cons, but he is not being guided by a quantitative balance of reasons, anyway; he is guided rather by the self-understanding that he gains by bringing to consciousness how he thinks and feels about the alternatives – which he does by consciously having thoughts and feelings about them, not about his own thoughts and feelings.

✻　✻　✻

What was initially mere neglect of this possibility has recently become an article of positive doctrine among philosophers. For example:[15]

---

[15] Simon Blackburn, *Ruling Passions* (Oxford: Clarendon Press, 1998), 253–4. See also Mark Johnston's discussion of "the projectivist *epoche*" in "The

Typically, in deliberation what I ... pay attention to are the relevant features of the external world: the cost of the alternatives, the quality of the goods, the durability of the cloth, the fact that I made a promise. I don't also pay attention to my own desires.... Deliberation is an active engagement with the world, not a process of introspecting our own consciousness of it. The last thing you want to do when you are wondering when to make your dash through the traffic, or whether to move bishop to rook 5, is to take your mind off the traffic or the chessboard.

At first glance, this passage seems plausible. But I believe that it rests on a subtle confusion. The confusion is between thought and attention. True enough, deliberation is "an active engagement with the world" that generally does not involve introspection. But 'active engagement' and 'introspection' are terms that indicate where our attention is focused. To say that we are not introspecting is merely to say that our attention is not focused inwards; it is not to deny that we are conscious of what we are thinking – aware *that* we are thinking it – even as we attend to the external world. We are aware of our thoughts, but we don't attend to them.

The point is that even if we don't attend to our thoughts, our awareness of them can still be what connects them to our actions, just as Williams's background awareness of his thoughts was what held them together. In consciously thinking favorably of the cloth, or anxiously about the traffic, we have second-order awareness of our favor or our anxiety, and that awareness can govern our actions even though it is not lit up by our attention. Our attention is focused on the cloth or the traffic, but our actions needn't follow from what we are attending to; it can follow from what we thereby become tacitly aware of.

In fact, investing attention in our consciousness of thinking rather than in the thinking itself would tend to interfere with our ability to act accordingly. If an improvisational actor focused

Authority of Affect," *Philosophy and Phenomenological Research* 63 (2001): 181–214.

his mind on a thespian syllogism beginning with an inventory of his character's attitudes and concluding with a judgment of what it would make sense for the character to do, he would be so distracted as to fall out of character. His attention must rather be focused on the words and actions of the other characters, and the idea for his next improvisational move must come to mind without mindful calculation. Even so, it must be calculated to make sense.

Making sense is even less likely to occupy the attention of an autonomous agent, whose explicit thinking must be done in full view of the audience consisting in himself. What would usually be most intelligible for him to do, in the eyes of that audience, is to pay undivided attention to the world around him, without worrying about what would be most intelligible. Paying attention to making sense would therefore be self-defeating, since it wouldn't make sense to him. If he is sad enough that it would make sense for him to cry, then it would also make sense for him to focus on whatever he's sad about rather than the question whether he's sad enough that it would make sense to cry.[16] But

---

[16] In some cases, what would make the most sense for an agent is not to entertain conscious thoughts about his external situation but to let go of self-awareness altogether. Someone who initially decided to swim with a flood of grief by having a cry may subsequently let himself sink back into that flood, forgetting himself in thoughts unaccompanied by the self-conscious "I think... ." Lost in thought about his troubles, he will no longer be enacting a conception of what it makes sense for him to do; and yet this departure from making sense may have been perfectly understandable. Self-enactment is not always the most intelligible mode of behavior. Sometimes it's more intelligible to let oneself grieve mindlessly, without acting out one's grief – which is just to say that perseverating in the exercise of rational agency is not always a rational thing to do.

There is also an intermediate stage between losing oneself in an activity and consciously putting it into action. Even when letting oneself get carried away by a behavior such as crying, one can be ready to pull up short if the behavior becomes discordant with one's thoughts. In this third case, one's thoughts and one's behavior proceed in parallel, connected only

even without attending to his sadness, he can still be aware of it and of what would make sense in light of it. And he can base his action on what he is tacitly aware of rather than what he's attending to.

On the one hand, then, the rational agent does not attend to the mechanics of self-enactment, any more than the improvisational actor attends to the mechanics of improvisation. On the other hand, the agent must not dissimulate about his action's being a self-enactment. If he does, he will end up in what Sartre called bad faith.

The paradigm case of bad faith for Sartre is the waiter who plays the role of a waiter as if it weren't a role – as if his inherent waiterliness were directly controlling his movements, whereas he is actually conforming those movements to his conception of the waiterly thing to do.[17] The waiter would not be in bad faith

---

counterfactually by one's readiness to stop if the two should diverge. As I suggested in the Introduction, one's practical thinking then functions like a theatrical prompter, following along in the script independently while standing ready to intervene if errors occur. The ability to think along with oneself in this way, with thoughts that neither follow nor lead one's behavior, depends on a degree of self-knowledge that can be attained only through long practice in the more deliberate, thought-first mode of action. It is a long-term accomplishment of rational agency.

I have discussed these issues further in "What Good Is a Will?," in *Action in Context*, ed. Anton Leist (Berlin/New York: de Gruyter, 2007), 193–215; and in "The Way of the Wanton."

[17] Jean-Paul Sartre, *Being and Nothingness; An Essay on Phenomenological Ontology*, trans. Hazel E. Barnes (New York: Philosophical Library, 1956), 59. Here I am not attempting an historically accurate interpretation of Sartre. I think that Sartre is less than clear about the nature of the waiter's bad faith. Sartre says that the waiter is in bad faith simply in virtue of "playing at being a waiter"; but he also points to the deliberately mechanical style of the waiter's movements as symptomatic of his bad faith. As I see

if he let go of self-awareness and fell back on his professional habits and skills, proceeding on "automatic pilot,"[18] or if he enacted the part of a waiter candidly, by playing a self-enacting waiter who is admittedly fitting his behavior to a conception of what a waiter would do. What lands him in bad faith is that he plays the part of a waiter who isn't playing the part.

In bad faith, or any other form of inauthenticity, the agent ends up acting on a false conception of what he is doing, and so he fails at practical reasoning, as I conceive it. For as I conceive it, practical reasoning aims at self-understanding, which the agent can attain by enacting a conception of what he is doing, but only if that conception will be true of its own enactment. A false self-conception inevitably yields self-misunderstanding, which frustrates practical reasoning, according to my view.

My view of agency, though now fraught with theory, corresponds to the bare phenomenological contrast that I drew between crying as an action and crying as a fit of passion. Crying as a fit of passion simply manifests its motivating emotion, I said, whereas the action manifests that emotion under the guidance of one's conception of crying. All that I have now added by way of theory is an explanation of how the behavioral manifestations of an emotion can be guided by such a conception and what that process amounts to – namely, acting for a reason.

An objection to my explanation is that it misrepresents the sense in which a rational agent seeks to do the intelligible thing, or the thing that makes sense. The claim that a rational agent

it, this simulated automaticity shows, not that the man is playing at being a waiter, but rather that he is playing at being a waiting-machine – that is, something that does what a waiter does but without enacting an idea of it.

[18] In this case, he resembles the agent described in the first paragraph of footnote 16.

seeks to do what makes sense is uncontroversial if "what makes sense" means what's appropriate or right or best, or what seems so from the agent's perspective. Yet I understand the phrase in a purely cognitive sense meaning "what is explicable in folk-psychological terms," a sense in which it is hardly an uncontroversial description of what a rational agent seeks to do. I thus seem to be trading on an equivocation.

I'm not equivocating, though; I'm deliberately changing the subject. Whereas most philosophers think that the intelligibility of an action derives from its appropriateness or rightness or goodness, real or perceived, I am going to argue that appropriateness or rightness or goodness derives from intelligibility – which cannot then derive from such normative considerations, on pain of circularity. My reason for thus reversing the order of explanation is that I can thereby account for what is less clear, normativity, in terms of what is more clear, psychological explanation, whereas the alternative is to leave normativity as the unexplained term, with uncertain prospects for explaining it.[19]

*   *   *

A second objection to my view of practical reasoning is that it casts self-understanding as the ultimate aim of every action, thereby giving all of our practical affairs an oddly theoretical orientation. This objection misinterprets my view.

The aims of our actions, according to my view, are whatever they ordinarily seem to be: pleasure, health, friendship, chocolate. Self-understanding is not an aim ulterior to these aims – not something for the sake of which we pursue them. It is rather an aim with respect to our manner of pursuing these and other aims, which we pursue for their own sakes. In this respect, self-understanding is like efficiency. We cannot pursue efficiency alone; we can pursue it only in the course of pursuing other

[19] Other reasons for my methodology are discussed in Lecture 5.

aims, by seeking to pursue them efficiently. And in seeking to pursue them efficiently, we don't pursue them for the sake of efficiency; we pursue them for themselves, albeit with the additional aim of doing so efficiently. Efficiency will never be our ultimate aim, then, even if we strive for it in everything we do. So it is with self-understanding.

Fortunately, pursuing pleasure, pursuing health, and so on are intelligible things to do, and so our drive toward self-understanding ratifies and reinforces those pursuits. When I say that these pursuits are rational because they're intelligible, keep in mind that they're intelligible, in the first place, only because pleasure, health, and so on are things that we want. It is because of wanting them that we pursue them, albeit in a manner regulated for intelligibility.

I thus imagine the drive toward self-understanding as exerting a fairly minor, modulating role in our practical affairs. It influences which desired objects we choose to pursue, how we harmonize them with one another, organize our efforts toward them, and express our thoughts and feelings along the way. Like method actors, we never stop relying on our first-order impulses as motives for our activities; we merely shape those activities into the most understandable enactment of our impulses, all considered, while also shaping those impulses, over time, so as to make them more intelligible to enact.

Here is a third objection: my view appears to mistake the sense in which reasoning can be practical. According to this objection, practical reasoning should be practical both subjectively, in its explicit topic, and objectively, in the functional role that it plays. I seem to assign practical reasoning the oddly impractical topic of what would be the psychologically intelligible thing to do, along with the equally impractical function of producing psychological self-understanding. The objection is that practical reasoning should address the practical question what *to* do, and it should thereby serve the practical function of guiding us toward what is *to be done*.

In order to consider this objection, we should start with a neutral characterization of the questions that practical reasoning should address. Practical reasoning, let us say, should address questions whose resolution will entail the performance of actions, just as theoretical reasoning addresses questions whose resolution will entail the formation of beliefs. With respect to the subjective topic of practical reasoning, then, the issue is which question is such as to be resolved by the performance of an action.

The present objection assumes that the question to be resolved by the performance of an action is the question what to do. But this assumption is backward. Questions are not constituted as theoretical or practical by being explicitly about belief or action, asking what to believe or what to do, respectively; rather, belief and action are constituted by resolving, or being such as would resolve, the sort of questions addressed by their respective modes of reasoning.

The question that gets resolved by the formation of a belief is not *what to believe*; it is rather the question *what is true*, and being the actual or possible resolution of such a question is what makes something a belief. An attitude qualifies as a belief, that is, because it settles (or forestalls) the question what is true. To judge by this analogy, the question that gets resolved by the performance of an action should not be the question what to do; it should rather be a question such that resolving it constitutes something as an action, as the question what is true is the one whose resolution constitutes a belief. If we want to know which question is practical in the sense that it is resolved by an action, we need to consider, not which question is explicitly *about* action, but which question is such that being its actual or possible resolution is constitutive of *being* an action.[20] What I have argued in

---

[20] Of course, there is a sense in which theoretical or practical reasoning can be described as being about what to believe or what to do, simply in virtue of being such as to conclude in a belief or an action. But I am discussing

this lecture, by comparing an agent to an improvisational actor, is that the question whose resolution constitutes an action is the question what it makes sense to do. (I will expand on this argument in Lecture 5.)

✳ ✳ ✳

So much for the subjective topic of practical reasoning; what about its objective function? Shouldn't practical reasoning be of some practical use to us? And what practical use is there in reasoning about which action would be intelligible in psychological terms?

I grant that there is a sense of the term 'practical reasoning' that means "practically useful reasoning," like the sense of 'practical shoes' that means "practically useful shoes." Many kinds of reasoning are practical in this sense, including instrumental reasoning about how to produce particular results that happen to be desired. But I am using the term 'practical reasoning' in the sense that means "reasoning that concludes with an action" and indeed "reasoning such that being its (actual or possible) conclusion is what makes something an action" – in other words, reasoning that defines the realm of the practical rather than reasoning that has a function within that realm.

In fact, I have said nothing about the practical functions that might be served by the reasoning that I call practical. I have spoken only about its explicit topic – the question that it seeks to answer – as well as its role in constituting behaviors as actions. If it has any practical functions, they would be the functions for which it was designed, presumably by evolution, the functions by performing which it contributed to the reproductive fitness

the explicit topic of each mode of reasoning, the question that is explicitly under consideration. For a discussion of deliberation about what to believe, see Nishi Shah and J. David Velleman, "Doxastic Deliberation," *Philosophical Review* 114 (2005): 497–534.

of our ancestors. And there is no reason to assume that these functions can be read off its explicit topic. What was contributed to the fitness of our ancestors by reasoning about what it would make sense to do need not have been self-understanding.

Reasoning about what it would make sense to do arose, I believe, from the combination of two capacities – theoretical inquiry and objective self-awareness – each of which would have been adaptive in its own right. The mode of reasoning that arose when they were combined may have produced fortuitous advantages that cannot be read off its topics or procedures. Then again, it may not have produced any additional advantages at all. According to Kant, if Mother Nature had been looking out for our interests, she might have designed us to be governed by instinct rather than a will.[21]

* * *

One last objection. My view of practical reasoning seems to count an agent's admitted vices – laziness, for example – as prima facie reasons for undesirable actions – say, procrastinating – because they render such actions intelligible. Here considerations of what's intelligible seem to diverge from considerations of what would be best, and so they seem to diverge from genuine reasons for acting as well.

But why does the agent in this example think of himself as lazy rather than as laid-back or easygoing? The former self-description seems to express reflective disapproval, perhaps arising from the agent's perception that his laziness conflicts with many of his own ambitions and values. Those conflicts are bound to cloud the question of which courses of action he has sufficient enthusiasm to undertake, and hence which courses would make sense for him. In the context of a self-conception that includes a self-attribution of laziness, the way to make best sense to himself

---

[21] I expand on this point in "What Good Is a Will?"

may be, not to procrastinate, but to look for more robust and reliable sources of motivation, which can decisively resolve the conflicts and, with them, the confusion about what it makes sense to do. This resolution won't be needed by an agent who has no ambitions or values to be frustrated by his laziness; but such an agent is more likely to describe himself, and to be described by others, as laid-back or easygoing.[22] And the rational course for an easygoing agent may well be to go easy. Thus, my view of practical reasoning doesn't necessarily recommend procrastination for this agent, unless he is of a type for whom procrastinating would indeed seem like the rational thing to do.

Keep in mind that self-understanding is not simply a matter of making sense *of* oneself as one is; it is also a matter of making sense *to* oneself, perhaps by being otherwise. Granted, an agent in whom lethargy and ambition are continually at odds may well understand just how deeply conflicted he is and why he is continually vacillating between lying back and pressing ahead. But this self-understanding is more complicated and clouded than that which is available to an unconflicted agent, for whom there is a single course that it would clearly make sense to take. The conflicted agent would therefore clarify his life – clarify himself to himself – by becoming less conflicted, if he can.[23]

Practical reasoning can thus favor self-reform for an agent who thinks he is lazy, if the frustration of his ambitions, and the

---

[22] This example illustrates a phenomenon that I discussed earlier. In thinking of himself as lazy, the agent thinks only about his laziness, but he thinks about it disapprovingly, and insofar as his thinking is conscious, it makes him aware of his disapproval as well. As I have argued, philosophical accounts of practical reasoning tend to limit themselves to the explicit content of the agent's thoughts and neglect what he expresses to himself by thinking them, whereby he makes more than their explicit content available to his self-understanding.

[23] I discuss this issue further in "Willing the Law," in *Practical Conflicts: New Philosophical Essays*, ed. Peter Baumann and Monika Betzler (Cambridge: Cambridge University Press, 2004), 27–56, reprinted in *Self to Self*, 284–311.

resulting confusion, would make it intelligible for him to take the trouble of turning over a new leaf. Note that in this case, practical reasoning will work in two distinct ways. On the one hand, an alternative self-conception would give him access to better self-understanding, if only he could live up to it; on the other hand, reforming himself in order to live up to that better self-understanding may be something that it makes sense to do. An alternative possibility arises, however: that although a particular agent would make more sense to himself after turning over a new leaf, he cannot make sense of taking the steps required to turn it. Maybe the effort required to become less lazy would make no sense for him, given how lazy he is.

If reforming his vices wouldn't make sense for him as he is, given those vices, the agent may find himself in what might be called a rational dead end, from which he can see a more rational place to be but no rational way of getting there. I regard this consequence as a virtue of my view rather than a flaw. It helps to explain why Aristotle was right to emphasize the importance of a good upbringing: a good upbringing is, among other things, an induction into a self-conception that won't lead into rational dead ends.[24]

This concludes my account of agency and practical reasoning. In the next lecture, I will extend this account from reasoning about actions to reasoning about reactions – reasoning, that is, about how to feel. When our feelings toward something are based on a reason, I will say, we are not just reacting to it but valuing it. And the reasons whose influence can thus transform reacting into valuing reveal the nature of value – a topic that will bring me closer to the topic of morality.

[24] *Nicomachean Ethics* 1095b, 1179b ff. I discuss rational dead ends, and a method for escaping them, in "Motivation By Ideal," *Philosophical Explorations* 5 (2002): 89–104, reprinted in *Self to Self,* 312–29.

2

Reacting

There are people whom I like despite knowing that they aren't very likeable, and then there are people whom I know to be likeable even though I just don't like them. Similarly, there are some jokes that I laugh at while judging that they aren't funny, and other jokes in which I can see the humor without being at all disposed to laugh. But when I say that I *find* someone likable, or *find* something funny, I indicate that I am doing some third thing. On the one hand, I am not just liking or laughing; I am discovering – "finding" – some quality that merits a response. On the other hand, I am not simply judging that the relevant quality is present; I am finding it with the relevant sensibility, precisely by responding affectively rather than judging. I am detecting likeability or humorousness with the appropriate detector, namely, liking or laughter.

To find someone likeable or admirable or enviable, to find something interesting or amusing or disgusting – these are what might be called *guided responses*, responses that are somehow sensitive to indications of their own appropriateness. Guided responses are not value judgments, since they are still conative or affective rather than cognitive attitudes. But they resemble judgments in being regulated for appropriateness, and so they are more than mere responses. Finding someone likeable is more judgmental than merely liking him, but it need not entail passing judgment on his likeability. It is rather a matter of liking him in a way that is sensitive to what makes him worth liking. We can mark the partial similarity of such guided responses to value judgments, or evaluations, by describing them as instances of *valuing*.

This analysis of valuing now resembles my analysis of action in the previous lecture. According to that analysis, action differs from mere bodily movement in virtue of being performed for reasons. Bumping into someone, for example, can be an accidental bodily movement, but if one bumps into him for a reason, then it's not just a movement but an action. This analysis of action can be taken as a clue to the nature of reasons for acting. It implies that reasons for acting are considerations such that, when bodily movement is regulated in accordance with them, it rises to the status of action. That is, reasons are considerations whose regulatory influence can make the difference between an accidental collision and a shove.

My analysis of valuing offers a similar clue about reasons for valuing. I have said that finding someone likeable is not just liking him but liking him in a manner sensitive to whatever makes liking him appropriate. But if anything makes liking him appropriate, then it qualifies as a reason for liking him. To find someone likeable is thus to like him for a reason. What makes for the guided response that amounts to valuing, in other words, is that the response is guided to its target by reasons. And the relevant reasons are those considerations whose guidance would make the difference between merely responding to it and valuing it – between, say, liking someone and finding him likeable, or laughing at something and finding it funny.[1]

If my next step were to say that reasons for liking someone consist precisely in his likeability – that reasons for valuing

---

[1] Here I am ignoring the case of acting or responding for bad reasons, which do not actually make the action or response appropriate. The case of bad reasons must be analyzed in terms of good ones, which must therefore be analyzed first.

something, in general, consist in its value – then my analysis would be fairly pointless. No philosophical work would have been done, since "value" is the term most in need of analysis. My aim is rather to fill that need, by proposing the opposite order of constitution. Something's being valuable, I want to say, consists in there being reasons for valuing it, which are considerations whose regulatory influence would turn a brute reaction to it into an instance of valuing. Whatever it is about someone consideration of which would guide us to like him in a way that amounted not just to liking him but to finding him likeable – *that* is what constitutes likeability. Likeability, in other words, is that whose detection, in the form of liking, amounts to finding someone likeable rather than merely liking him; humorousness is that whose detection with laughter amounts to finding something humorous rather than merely laughing at it.

The question, then, is how responses are regulated when they are more than casual or haphazard. What is guided laughter or guided liking? Answering this question, and using the answer to illuminate the nature of value, make up the business of the present lecture.[2]

A process that guides our reactions has been observed in a field of social psychology called attribution theory. As it turns out, our reactions are guided by considerations very much like the ones that guide our actions, according to my account of practical reasoning.

In one experiment, when male subjects were approached by an attractive female interviewer on a long, wobbly footbridge

---

[2] The theory of value presented here bears many similarities to a theory presented by Elizabeth Anderson in *Value in Ethics and Economics* (Cambridge, MA: Harvard University Press, 1993).

over a 230-foot-deep canyon, they showed greater signs of being attracted to her – were more likely to telephone her afterward for a promised debriefing, for example – than subjects approached by the same interviewer on a solid wooden bridge further upstream.[3] These subjects appear to have perceived their anxiety as attraction and acted on that perception. The converse effect has also been demonstrated: subjects are less likely to report or display an emotional response if they have been given an alternative explanation for its symptoms. For example, shy people placed in a socially awkward situation do not feel or act shy if they have been told that they are being exposed to an invisible stimulant that tends to cause jitters and sweaty palms.[4]

How does this attribution mechanism work? Attribution theorists generally explain it in terms of a drive toward self-understanding – or, as they prefer to say, toward "cognitive consistency." This cognitive drive gives us a strong incentive to react in ways that we can explain in light of the circumstances, and to behave in ways that we can explain in light of our reaction. Feeling stirred, we look to our circumstances to suggest an interpretation, and we then behave accordingly. In doing so, we can shape an inchoate disturbance into a specific response, or transform one response into another.

Initially we may feel excitations that could be symptomatic, say, of nervousness, fear, or awe. Which of these responses we

---

[3] Donald G. Dutton and Arthur P. Aron, "Some Evidence for Heightened Sexual Attraction under Conditions of High Anxiety," *Journal of Personality and Social Psychology* 30 (1974): 510–17. I review related research in "From Self-Psychology to Moral Philosophy," *Philosophical Perspectives* 14 (2000): 349–77, reprinted in *Self to Self* (New York: Cambridge University Press, 2006), 224–52. Among my claims in that paper is that various disagreements among researchers in this field – which I am glossing over here – are based on misunderstandings that obscure broad areas of agreement.

[4] S. E. Brodt and P.G. Zimbardo, "Modifying Shyness-related Social Behavior through Symptom Misattribution," *Journal of Personality and Social Psychology* 41 (1981): 437–49.

interpret ourselves as having depends on which response would make sense to us under the circumstances; how we go on to behave depends on how it would make sense for us to behave, given the response we interpret ourselves as having; and we thereby give our initially ambiguous feelings the stamp of nervousness, fear, or awe, depending on which would maximize the overall intelligibility of situation, self, and behavior.

Why do our excitations come to fulfill our interpretation of them? The reason is that our actions feed back into their psychological sources both causally and conceptually. Fearful actions can turn our response into fear partly by shaping the response itself, in the way that smiling has been shown to affect our mood.[5] Fearful actions can also help to constitute which response we are having, since part of what makes the difference between nervousness and fear is how it is manifested in behavior.

The self-fulfilling effect of these self-attributions enables to choose our responses to some extent. Rather than accept our response as fear, we can say, "I refuse to be afraid," meaning that we are interpretively marshalling our excitations into awe or nervousness – or perhaps even shyness – by crediting ourselves with one of those attitudes and following suit in our behavior. If we succeed in making the alternative interpretation stick, then we may indeed have implemented a decision as to our response.

Having noted this way of regulating our responses, we need look no further, I suggest, for the kind of regulation that turns

[5] See J. D. Laird, "The Real Role of Facial Responses in Experience of Emotion: A Reply to Tourangeau and Ellsworth, and Others," *Journal of Personality and Social Psychology* 47 (1984): 909–17; S. E. Duclos, J. D. Laird, E. Schneider, M. Sexter, L. Stern, and O. Van Lighten, "Emotion-specific Effects of Facial Expressions and Postures on Emotional Experience," *Journal of Personality and Social Psychology* 57 (1989): 100–8.

our emotional responses into valuations rather than brute reactions.[6] Just as behaving becomes acting when it is regulated by the agent's conception of what it would make sense for him to do, so reacting becomes valuing when it is regulated by the subject's conception of what it would make sense for him to feel. The upshot of the analogy is that considerations of intelligibility are reasons for valuation as well as for action. The considerations whose influence turns reaction into valuation are reasons for valuing, and they turn out to be considerations of intelligibility. So the considerations that make something valuable, by providing reasons to value it, are considerations in light of which valuing it makes sense.

This suggestion will be met with the objection that I have reversed the order of explanation between appropriateness and intelligibility.[7] What makes a response appropriate cannot be that it is intelligible, according to this objection, because what makes it intelligible, to begin with, can only be that it is appropriate.[8] I am well aware of reversing the explanatory order in this way. I do so without apology, on the methodological grounds that it assigns to the explanandum that term which is more in need of explanation.

---

[6] For an insightful description of this process as it may take place in child development, see Barbara Herman, *Moral Literacy* (Cambridge, MA: Harvard University Press, 2007), 13–18.

[7] In "The Authority of Affect" (*Philosophy and Phenomenological Research* 63 [2001]: 181–214), Mark Johnston argues that the positive or negative affect involved in a desire can render its motivational force intelligible by presenting its object as "appealing" or "repellent." I am not speaking of intelligibility in this sense; I am speaking instead of the psychological-explanatory intelligibility of a response, in light of its role in a person's mental economy.

[8] See, for example, John McDowell, "Values and Secondary Qualities," in *Morality and Objectivity: A Tribute to J. L. Mackie,* ed. Ted Honderich (London: Routledge & Kegan Paul, 1985), 110–29.

This methodology is especially helpful, I think, in accounting for the subtle shades of objectivity and subjectivity in our values. On the one hand, the conditions of appropriateness for a response appear to depend on the sensibility that is capable of it. What makes something appropriate to admire depends somehow on what an admiring sensibility is attuned to, which is what tends to elicit admiration from a sensibility equipped for that response. On the other hand, the conditions of appropriateness for a response cannot be read off the actual responses of the relevant sensibility. What's appropriate to admire isn't merely what admiring subjects actually do admire. So how can what's admirable depend on the responsiveness of an admiring sensibility without collapsing into whatever actually elicits the admiring response?

This problem comes in varying degrees. To begin with, some things just aren't likeable or admirable, and their lack of likeability or admirability seems to be independent of the subject's perspective. But then we allow for individual differences of taste, which entail that what is likeable or admirable for me needn't be so for you. Even these person-relative values seem to transcend the actual responses of the relevant persons, however, since my likes and dislikes can fail to detect what is really likeable from my perspective. Then again, you and I can criticize one another's sensibilities as needing cultivation or refinement, as if there were an objective criterion of good taste. And yet different values appear to differ in their susceptibility to such a criterion, since we allow more leeway for tastes in liking than in admiration.

How can the conditions of appropriateness for a response be objective in some cases and relative to individual sensibilities in others, while also allowing for rational criticism of those sensibilities, and to different degrees for different responses? The answer, I suggest, is that the fundamental standard of appropriateness for a response is its intelligibility, which is determined partly by the psychological nature of the response itself and partly by differences among individual sensibilities, which can themselves be compared and criticized on grounds of intelligibility.

*　*　*

Consider what makes it intelligible to admire someone. Admiration has a distinctive functional role: it disposes one to emulate the admired person, to defer to him, and to approve of his words and actions. In acquiring these dispositions, one may become either more or less intelligible to oneself, depending on one's other attitudes – beliefs with which the person's opinions may harmonize or clash; ideals that he may or may not exemplify; interests that he may or may not share; likes and dislikes of other people whom he may resemble.

If someone falls short of one's own ideals or ambitions, specializes in what seem like trivialities, espouses what seem like idiocies, reminds one of a hated foe, and resembles no one else whom one admires, then admiring him would make no sense, and in two respects. First, it's hard to explain why one would acquire a disposition to emulate and defer to someone of that kind; and second, acquiring that disposition would make it hard to figure out how it made sense to behave. Would it make sense to emulate the person's failure in the very pursuits at which one otherwise hoped to succeed? Would it make sense to defer to his judgments contradicting one's deepest beliefs? These questions would have no clear and uncomplicated answers, if one really came to admire him. One would be like the conflicted procrastinator considered in the previous lecture, who had no clear path to any of his options. In short, one would make less sense to oneself admiring him than not admiring him. That's why he isn't admirable, whether or not one admires him in fact.

As this example illustrates, the criterion of appropriateness for a response is holistically interdependent with those for other responses, as are the corresponding values. Whether it makes sense to admire someone who excels at a pursuit to which one has hitherto been indifferent may depend on whether it makes sense to begin taking an interest in that pursuit – which may of course depend on whether it makes sense in other respects to admire the person. Similarly, a state of excitation may need to be diagnosed as either fear or awe or nervousness, but it is unlikely to be all three at once. What's frightening may therefore depend on what's awesome or unnerving, and vice versa. That is, what it makes sense to interpret as, and thereby resolve into, awe may depend on what it makes sense to treat as fear or nervousness instead.

Sometimes, different responses may be naturally incompatible. Fear, anger, ennui, and disgust tend to dampen amusement, and so it can be difficult to understand why we are laughing at things that would ordinarily frighten, offend, bore, or sicken us.[9] We say, "That's not funny," though sometimes we are laughing as we say it; and then we may add, "So why am I laughing?" This rhetorical question confirms that the unfunny is that which we don't understand laughing at. The reason why we don't understand laughing at something is not that it is unfunny; rather, we don't understand laughing at it because it's boring or offensive or disgusting – or utterly unlike the other things that amuse us – and the resulting incongruousness of laughing at it is the reason why we think it isn't funny, despite our laughter.

Thus, what it makes sense to be amused by depends in part on what it makes sense to be disgusted, bored, or offended by. And each of these latter responses has its own functional profile, determining how it fits into our self-understanding, perhaps in conjunction with yet other responses. What's admirable or

---

[9] I don't mean to deny the possibility of sick or offensive humor. But these forms of humor usually work by testing the limits of the disgusting or offensive; they fall flat as soon as they cause genuine disgust or offense. We laugh partly out of surprise at what we can see or hear without becoming sick or angry; beyond that point, the laughing stops.

desirable may therefore bear indirectly on what's amusing, by way of what is or isn't boring.

These examples illustrate, further, the idiosyncratic nature of responses and the corresponding values. What it makes sense for me to admire is not necessarily what it makes sense for you to admire, in light of the functional-explanatory connections between admiration and other responses such as belief, desire, love, hate, fear, and awe, in which you and I may also differ. Each of us can thus have sensibilities in light of which things can be valuable for one of us without necessarily being valuable for the other, because valuing them makes sense for one but not for both.

Idiosyncrasy has its limits, however. There are many responses that all of us tend to have by virtue of our shared human nature. Such nearly universal responses include: an array of physiological appetites; an aversion to pain, separation, and frustration; an inclination toward pleasure, connection, and the fluid exercise of skill; the inborn and automatic fight-or-flight response; an interest in the human face and form; an initial dislike of snakes, spiders, blood, and the dark; and so on. Given the holism of what makes sense in our responses, these fixed points of human nature constrain most if not all of our values. Some things are desirable for any human being, because desiring them will make sense for anyone; other things simply cannot be desirable, because desiring them won't make sense for anyone. That's not to say that everyone desires the former and doesn't desire the latter; rather, it's to say that everyone would make more sense to himself desiring the former and not desiring the latter, given his natural endowment as a member of the species.

The fixed points of human nature place different degrees of constraint on the intelligibility of different responses. Disgust is directly plugged in to the physiological reactions of gagging and retching; desire is regularly sparked by the appetites, but it can also flare up independently, in response to just about anything; there may be nothing that human nature determines us to admire, and yet admiration is deeply embedded in the network of other attitudes; whereas amusement mostly floats free of the network, except for the few connections through which it is inhibited by fear, disgust, anger, and boredom. What makes sense by way of each response is consequently more or less constrained, depending on its degree of natural connectivity.

I believe that the previously noted shades of objectivity and subjectivity can be explained by these considerations – idiosyncratic differences in how it makes sense to respond, commonalities based in our shared nature, the possibility of responding incongruously and of cultivating more intelligible responses. As the intelligibility of a response is more closely tied to our individual characters, the response is susceptible to more specific guidance from a personal standard of appropriateness; as the intelligibility of a response is more closely tied to our shared nature, the response is susceptible to more specific guidance from an interpersonal standard; and a standard of appropriateness may itself be improved, as the corresponding sensibility is rendered more intelligible.

A sensibility can become more intelligible, for example, by following recognizable regularities. Practical reasoning therefore favors cultivating appreciative responses to things that belong to general kinds – kinds that are recognizable, if not by explicit description, then at least by family resemblance. Whatever makes it intelligible for me to laugh at a particular joke – thereby making the joke amusing, at least for me – would make it intelligible for me to laugh at any relevantly similar joke, which would therefore qualify as amusing for me, too.[10] Insofar as I can

---

[10] On a particular occasion, of course, the relevant similarity may not be an intrinsic quality of the joke itself: what makes it intelligible for me to laugh

generalize about what kinds of jokes amuse me, or what kinds of people I admire, I can better understand why I am laughing at a particular joke or emulating a particular person.

Practical reason thus encourages me to identify kinds of jokes, recognizable by family resemblance if not by description, that constitute what is amusing for me. It thereby pushes me toward a position that appears to confirm the view that being amusing-for-me is a real, descriptive property of things. The reason why amusingness-for-me comes to seem like a real property, however, is that I have cultivated a sense of humor that is regularly responsive to jokes of recognizable kinds, so that I can understand being amused, when I am amused. The same goes for my senses of admiration, inspiration, disgust, and so on: they have been cultivated under rational pressure to be responsive to recognizable kinds of things, which constitute what is admirable, inspiring, or disgusting for me.

The same pressure toward generality that leads an agent to identify what is amusing or admirable for him also leads him to cultivate values that are universal, in the sense that interests moral philosophers. Specifically, it leads him to cultivate values that

on this occasion may be that I'm drunk or nervous, which would make it intelligible for me to laugh at just about anything. Yet I am also under rational pressure to identify kinds of jokes that regularly tend to amuse me by themselves, so that I can comprehend my responses to jokes more generally, without reference to the circumstances. And a joke that's amusing for me on this occasion because I'm drunk or nervous may not be intrinsically amusing for me – not "really" amusing, I might say – because it is not the kind of joke that generally makes it intelligible for me to laugh, irrespective of the circumstances. This notion of what is "really" amusing (or desirable or admirable or whatever) solves a problem raised by Justin D'Arms and Daniel Jacobson in "The Moralistic Fallacy: On the 'Appropriateness' of Emotions," *Philosophy and Phenomenological Research* 61 (2000): 65–90.

do not make exceptions for himself, so that they can be shared with others.

Consider two people who are locked in a blood feud. Each conceives of himself as obliged to return the other's attacks, in order to deter him from mounting further attacks in the future; and each conceives of himself as implacably determined not to be deterred. Each thinks of the other's attacks as aggressive and his own as defensive; the other's as outrages and his own as vindications.

One might say that these characters are being prudentially irrational, because they are locked in a war that is worse for each than peace would be. But from their perspective, of course, their war is a prisoners' dilemma, in which each would be even worse off if he declared a cease-fire unilaterally.

I want to say something different about these characters. Each understands the other as susceptible to deterrence, while understanding himself as not to be deterred; each thinks that it makes sense to be indomitable while trying to dominate the other. *These people don't have a good grasp of what they are up to.* They apply to themselves a special theory of human psychology, different from the one that they apply to people in general.

One might say: They understand themselves well enough; it's the other they don't understand. I say: They take themselves to be an exception to what they otherwise regard as psychological laws; how satisfactory a self-understanding can that be? After all, if they conceived of themselves as susceptible to deterrence, as they conceive of people in general, then they would actually be susceptible to deterrence, since being deterred would be what makes sense to them. They could thus unify their self-understanding with their understanding of human psychology, according to which people can be deterred. Alternatively, they could unify their understanding of human psychology with their understanding of themselves, by conceiving of people in general as resistant to being deterred – in which case, they would no longer see the point in retaliation. Either way, a self-understanding consistent with their understanding of human nature would lead them to break off the feud.

Thus, if we understand values as the properties or categories to which it makes sense to respond in particular ways, we can begin to see how values support a universalizing tendency characteristic of morality. And we can see how they support this tendency despite reflecting patterns of response that we improvise, in our capacity as rational agents.

Although my conception of value explains why we strive to value things consistently according to kinds, and consistently between valuers, such consistency is a rational desideratum, not a rational imperative such as would apply to our evaluative responses if they could reflect antecedent value-properties supervening on nature. Inconsistent valuing, in the form of conflicting or ambivalent responses, is to be deprecated as inimical to self-understanding, but it is not to be condemned as senseless or stupid. Let me conclude this lecture with one example.

The birth of a child can move us to value judgments that seem inconsistent. Consider, for example, a fourteen-year-old girl who decides to have a baby.[11] We think that the birth of a

---

[11] This case is discussed by Derek Parfit in *Reasons and Persons* (Oxford: Oxford University Press, 1984), Chapter 16. For a fuller discussion of the case, see Part 3 of my "Persons in Prospect," *Philosophy and Public Affairs* 36 (2008): 222–88. Also relevant to this discussion are: Caspar Hare, "Voices from Another World: Must We Respect the Interests of People Who Do Not, and Will Never, Exist?," *Ethics* 117 (2007): 498–523; Jeff McMahan, "Preventing the Existence of People with Disabilities," in David Wasserman, Jerome Bickenbach, and Robert Wachbroit (eds.), *Quality of Life and Human Difference: Genetic Testing, Health Care, and Disability* (New York: Cambridge University Press, 2005), 142–71; Larry Temkin, "Intransitivity and the Mere Addition Paradox," *Philosophy and Public Affairs* 16 1987: 138–87;

child to a fourteen-year-old mother will be unfortunate, even tragic, and hence that she should not decide to have one. But after the birth, we are loath to say that the child should not have been born. Indeed, we now think that the birth is something to celebrate – once a year, on the child's birthday.

We may be tempted to say that we have simply changed our minds in light of better information. Before the birth, we didn't know how things would turn out, and now we know more. But the birth did not bring to light any previously unknown information relevant to our judgments.[12] Or, at least, I mean to restrict my attention to cases in which it didn't. There may be cases in which we feared specific calamities, such as a birth defect or a descent into juvenile delinquency; and then if such possibilities don't materialize, we change our minds. I am not speaking of such cases; I am speaking of cases in which we disapproved of the girl's decision for reasons that are not falsified by subsequent developments, and yet we are subsequently glad about the birth. The child is raised under serious disadvantages of the very sort that we anticipated, but the severely disadvantaged child is still a child to be cherished.

We knew in advance how we would feel. Even as we deplored the girl's decision, we knew that we would welcome the child. We may even have cited this prospect to ourselves as a reason for softening our opinion: "Don't condemn her for deciding to have a child," we might have said: "Once it is born, you'll be delighted." But such arguments could not dispel our sense that something was wrong.

One might think that these judgments can be reconciled, after all, because their objects are not the same. When we think that the girl should not have a baby, the object of our judgment is

and Bernard Williams's paper "Consistency and Realism," *Proceedings of the Aristotelian Society* Supplementary Volume 40 (1966): 1–22.

[12] McMahan makes the same point in "Preventing the Existence of People with Disabilities," p. 155.

a quantified proposition, about her having some baby or other, whereas it is the birth of a particular baby that we will celebrate. And of course we can consistently think that her having *a* baby is unfortunate in general but not in the case of her having some particular one, since the general rule affirmed by our first judgment may allow for an exception noted by the second.

Yet the attempted reconciliation appears to be blocked by the fact, which was known to us in advance, that any baby she had would be welcomed. How can we judge that a fourteen-year-old's having a baby would be unfortunate as a rule, if we also judge that any particular instance of the rule would be an exception?

I do not think that we actually change our minds after the birth of this child, if a change of mind would entail giving up our antecedent judgment. We still think that the girl should not have had a baby, delighted though we are with the baby she has had. That one judgment predominated beforehand and the other afterward should not be allowed to obscure the fact that we are of two minds about the case.

One might hope to dispel the appearance of inconsistency by claiming that the former is a prima facie judgment, deploring any birth only insofar as the mother was underage and thus leaving open the possibility of mitigating circumstances. But we don't just think that the girl should not have had a baby insofar as she is underage; we think that she should not have had a baby all things considered; and yet we are glad about the birth of this baby all things considered as well.

The mother herself may regret her decision. She may wish that she hadn't had a baby, may believe that she shouldn't have had one. But of course she still loves the baby and is thankful that it was born. As in our case, her judgments persist in light of one another. That is, she regrets having had a baby when she did even though it was this baby; and she is thankful for this baby even though she had it when she did.

This conundrum is one of several that Derek Parfit considers in Part IV of *Reasons and Persons,* the part devoted to "Future Generations." I want to suggest a solution that Parfit doesn't consider. Parfit's entire discussion presupposes that our value judgments must be consistent as descriptions of the things they evaluate: they must be satisfiable by some distribution of positive and negative values across the possibilities. I think that the present case gives us reason to reject this assumption.

How could it be rational to have such different attitudes toward one and the same event? The answer lies in the different modes of presentation under which the event is viewed.

Our unfavorable judgment is about the baby under a description. What makes this judgment tenable despite our countervailing judgment is not, as we initially suspected, that it is general rather than singular. We think not just that the girl should not have had *a* baby at 14 but that she should not have had *the* baby she had at 14, thus considered under a definite description that picks it out uniquely. The reason why these judgments withstand our favorable judgment about the baby is that, whereas they rely on descriptions, the favorable judgment is about the baby considered demonstratively, as "this baby," "him," or "her."

Why does it matter whether we can make judgments about the baby considered demonstratively? The reason is that such judgments are guided by emotions that depend on acquaintance-based thought. One such emotion is love.[13] In the context of its mother's love, the child is presented to her mind

---

[13] On the role of perception in love, see my "Love as a Moral Emotion," *Ethics* 109 (1999): 338–74, reprinted in *Self to Self,* 70–109; and "Beyond Price,"

as it is known to her directly via sight and touch. She does not love it under descriptions of the form "such-and-such a child" or "the so-and-so" or even as "Fred" or "Sue." The latter modes of presentation would have been available to her even if she had merely heard the child described or referred to by name, in which case she would have been in no position to love it. Unlike those modes of presentation, acquaintance-based thought is a way of being mentally in touch or *en rapport* with an object; and the rapport it entails is prerequisite to the emotion of love.[14]

Our mental relation to something can determine which attitudes toward it make sense. Before we are acquainted with a baby, we can approve or disapprove of it, but loving it is quite impossible, in my view, and hence not intelligible, either; whereas loving a baby after being acquainted with it is the easiest thing in the world – intelligible, too.

The different responses that it makes sense to have toward the baby, as we think of it under different modes of presentation, account for our different value judgments about its birth. We should feel free to experience these responses and to hold the corresponding judgments, because value is the shadow of such attitudes, not an independent standard of their

Ethics 118 (2008): 191–212. I briefly summarize my conception of love in Lecture 4, below.

[14] Thus, an expectant mother who says that she already loves her future child may not be speaking the truth, in philosophical strictness. She may be imagining how she will love the child, mentally simulating what it will be like to love the child, or having fantasies of loving it. But until she becomes acquainted with it, her emotion cannot be love.

When does a prospective mother become acquainted with her child? I would say that she becomes acquainted with it when she first perceives it. And when does she first perceive her child? I would say that she perceives the child at the point traditionally called quickening, when the fetus begins to make movements that she can feel. Thus, the tradition that interpreted quickening to be a morally relevant threshold was not just a superstition, in my view; it drew what may indeed be a morally relevant distinction.

correctness. If the attitudes make sense, then the fact that they cast conflicting shadows cannot undermine their authority. And they make sense, despite the conflict between their shadows, because their intentional objects are different in ways that rationally affect the emotions informing our judgments.[15]

* * *

The child may see his mother's regret, and as he approaches adulthood, he may find the words for what he sees. "You wish you hadn't had a baby when you were so young, don't you?" If the mother is wise enough to realize that she cannot hide her feelings, her answer will be "Yes." "So you wish that I hadn't been born?" No, not at all.

---

[15] This dissolution of the problem would be unnecessary if our emotions led us to judgments positing distinct and incomparable values. If we judged merely that the girl's initial decision was imprudent, whereas the baby is beautiful, then we could interpret our judgments as descriptions satisfiable in the one and only actual world, on the grounds that beauty has nothing to do with prudence.

But I am imagining us as drawing – as I think we do draw – all-things-considered conclusions about whether a baby, or this baby, should have been brought into existence. And I am imagining that, whereas we still think that the girl shouldn't have had the baby she did, we think otherwise about this baby's having been born. Pluralism about value won't render these judgments compatible.

Parfit considers other ways of dealing with the conflict, but none strikes me as satisfactory. For example, Parfit claims that, were he the child of a birth that was unfortunate when viewed prospectively, he would agree in retrospect that he shouldn't have been born. I think that he might indeed hold this judgment, but I think that he would also be glad to have been born, so that the former judgment doesn't settle the issue.

I also prefer this solution to the one favored by McMahan, according to which we change our minds about the girl's decision to have a baby. McMahan considers a solution like mine, when discussing the evaluative import of "attachments to particulars," but he ultimately drops the solution in favor of one based on a change of mind.

What does the child's second question mean? He is asking whether his mother loves him and is thankful that he exists. What he wants to hear, in wanting to hear that she loves and cherishes him, is that she loves and cherishes him as the child of her acquaintance, the child she sees and hears and held as a baby in her arms. He doesn't care how she feels about the child she had when she was 14, under that description. Let her regret having had the child so described, so long as he himself, as he is known to her directly, can still be sure of her love.

So the child's second question is a non sequitur, as he and his mother dimly realize, even if they cannot articulate it. She may say, "I only wish that I could have had you when I was older" – which will be true but not the whole truth. She doesn't merely wish that she could have had this child when she was older; she thinks, all things considered, that she shouldn't have had a child at all when she was so young.

The child may be similarly ambivalent about his own birth, considered under different modes of presentation. If he has grown up disadvantaged by his mother's immaturity, as I have imagined, he may conclude from his own experience that no child should be born to a fourteen-year-old mother. And yet he may have a healthy self-love that makes him thankful for having been born.

One might think that these judgments of the child's are made from different perspectives – the first from an impersonal perspective, the second from the child's self-interested point of view. But as I have now imagined him, the child makes his first judgment on behalf of any child who might be born to an underage mother, from the perspective of that child's interests. It is for the sake of such a child that he thinks it shouldn't have been born, but also for the sake of the same child, in his own case, that he is grateful for having been born. And he doesn't think, "No child should be born to an underage mother, except for me"; rather, he thinks, "No child should be born to an underage mother, but I'm still thankful that I was born."

I think that similarly conflicted reactions can arise in the parents of children who are born severely disabled. These parents are, so to speak, doomed to love a child such as it is regrettable to have or to be – regrettable, that is, when considered as such a child, not of course as this child. In this respect, the parents are caught in a bind partly created by their love for their own child, a bind of a sort that makes the birth of such a child all the more tragic. Similarly, a child born into unfortunate circumstances is doomed to be attached to a particular existence such as it is regrettable to have. As an adult, he may resent the fact that his inevitable self-attachment forces him to be thankful for having been given a life of such an unfortunate kind.

Obviously, all-things-considered judgments had better not conflict if they are to provide practical guidance. Before conceiving her child or carrying it beyond the point where abortion becomes unavailable, the girl had to choose one way or the other, and we may have been called upon to advise her. Under those circumstances, being of two minds would have been problematic.

Under those circumstances, however, grounds for ambivalence were lacking. Before the child existed, he was not available to be loved or valued in other acquaintance-based ways. The mother's potential love for her child, or his potential self-love, were not antecedent grounds for choosing to create him, since she could not choose to create *him* in particular, considered demonstratively, as he would subsequently be loved.[16] Her choice was not whether to create him but whether to create a child. And of course she should have waited to create a child until she was better prepared to care for it.

[16] See Matthew Hanser, "Harming Future People," *Philosophy and Public Affairs* 19 (1990): 47–70, p. 61.

Our conflicting value judgments are rationally tolerable because
they are retrospective and hence not action-guiding.[17] Given that
there is no longer any occasion to make a decision, we can afford
to hold conflicting judgments about the decision that was made.
The pragmatic drawbacks of ambivalence have fallen away, and
the only remaining drawback would be a need to make judgments
that reflect some real distribution of values among the former
options. In my view, however, there is no such distribution of values, and so ambivalence about the case can be perfectly rational.

My attempt to vindicate these seemingly inconsistent judgments
depends on the claim that they are based on a rational pair of
attitudes. Yet the attitudes themselves may seem irrational precisely because they support conflicting judgments about one and
the same event. How can it be rational for a person to be glad, all
things considered, about his mother's having done something
that he regards, all things considered, as regrettable?

My answer is that these attitudes are inconsistent only when
interpreted as attributing incompatible properties to the event
in question. Yet as I have explained in this lecture, the notion
that values are properties distributed consistently among things
or states of affairs is actually the reflection of a pattern into which
our evaluative responses tend to fall when regulated in accordance with reasons for responding, which are conditions in light

---

[17] I do not accept Allan Gibbard's conception of value judgments as hypothetical plans for what to do in the relevant agent's circumstances (*Thinking
How to Live* [Cambridge, MA: Harvard University Press, 2003]). Plans are
not evaluative, and evaluations are not plans. When the girl decided to have
a baby, the natural expression of her plan would have been "I'm going to
have a baby" – not "Having a baby is the thing for me to do." And if she had
said "Having a baby is the thing for me to do," a natural rejoinder would
have been "So are you going to have one?" – which would have been an
inquiry as to her plan.

of which a response would make sense. The ultimate criterion of appropriateness for an evaluative response is intelligibility, which can be characterized independently of any postulation of values and can therefore be constitutive of values instead.

Although the most intelligible responses are usually those which are consistent across recognizable kinds of things and coherent with our other responses, departures from this pattern can be more intelligible in isolated cases. After all, intelligibility is a holistic matter of overall explanatory coherence, which sometimes requires trade-offs between alternative marginal gains or losses. And because values are constituted by intelligible responses rather than vice versa, we should tolerate cases in which the most intelligible responses cannot be modeled by a consistent distribution of values: they are simply cases in which the normal pattern of intelligibility doesn't hold.

As I have pointed out, conflicting attitudes can undermine intelligibility by making it difficult to identify an intelligible course of action. But in the case of procreative decisions, some of the most significant attitudes are essentially retrospective – such as love for a particular child, which is not available antecedently to guide the decision. It makes no sense to conceive a child out of love for it, an attitude that will not be possible until it exists. After the child exists, both thankfulness and regret may make sense as responses to it under different modes of presentation; and they may make sense all things considered, as parts of a holistically intelligible set of responses.

Consider again the parents of a severely disabled child. These parents may feel that if they truly love their child, as they unquestionably do, then they cannot lament the fact of having had a disabled child; and yet they cannot help lamenting what is unquestionably a lamentable fact. The resulting sense of emotional dissonance can wreak additional damage on the child and the family. In my view, however, there is no dissonance between the emotions themselves; the dissonance is between values that the emotions are mistakenly taken to reflect.

The parents should therefore forget about evaluating their child's existence and feel the emotions that clearly make sense for them to feel. What's intelligible in their responses may cast an inconsistent set of shadows on the world, but they are, after all, only shadows.

3

Interacting

What difference does it make in my attitude toward you, or what difference should it make, that I recognize you as a rational agent? Our answer to this question will depend on our conception of rational agency. According to the decision-theoretic conception, the recognition of your rational agency should lead me to do what would maximize my expected utility in light of what I expect you to do to maximize your expected utility in light of what you expect me to do. According to Kant, the recognition of your rational agency should lead me to respect you, by treating you never merely as a means but always also as an end in itself.

The question presupposes that I too am a rational agent. It asks not just how I should regard you upon recognizing you as a rational agent but how I as one rational agent should regard you upon recognizing you as another. According to my conception of rational agency, the answer is that I should regard you as a fellow self-enacting improviser. What would follow from regarding you in that way?

*   *   *

In recognizing you as a fellow self-enacter, I recognize that we share a perspective on one another's behavior. If I am to deal with you successfully, I need to understand your behavior, which is best understood in terms of your wants, plans, values, habits, emotions, traits of personality, and so on. And it is precisely because you need to understand yourself in similar terms that you are a rational agent. Although I don't share your egocentric perspective, then, we share a third-personal perspective from which you are, for both of us, a creature to be understood in folk-psychological terms. And of course we are in the corresponding position with respect to me. Each of us needs to understand both of us as creatures whose actions call for similar styles of explanation. As rational agents, you and I share a common stage, on which we improvise our own actions while viewing and seeking to interpret the actions of both.

Another thing that I recognize about you, in recognizing you as a rational agent, is that your behavior must be understood, at least in part, as enacting your conception of what it makes sense for you to do. When exercising your rational agency, you act under a self-interpretation, and I must interpret you as doing so, if I am to understand you. I won't really understand you, in other words, unless I understand how you understand yourself. I don't necessarily have to adopt your understanding of what you are doing, if I think you are mistaken about it – for example, if I think that you are deliberately crying while holding a false conception of yourself as helplessly overcome with grief.[1] Yet in order to interpret your very inauthenticity in such a case, I need to know what you take yourself to be doing, and so I need to know your interpretation in order to flesh out mine.[2]

---

[1] How could you cry deliberately if you conceived of yourself as crying involuntarily? The answer is that even the conception of yourself as crying involuntarily would have the effect that your *failing* to cry would be surprising and puzzling, and your crying would make more sense to you. The conception of yourself as crying involuntarily therefore inclines you to cry rather than not, although the resulting tears are not involuntary, and your self-understanding is therefore imperfect.

[2] As I mentioned in Lecture 1, inauthenticity involves acting on a false self-conception – a self-conception that one does not succeed in making true by acting on it. Although I think that every action of this kind is inauthentic,

Because your rational agency arises out of your need to understand yourself, I must assume that such inauthenticity on your part would constitute a failure of rationality, insofar as it would be a failure of self-understanding. Your rational agency militates against misunderstanding yourself. You have motives for self-deception, no doubt, but they are incidental to – indeed, inimical to – your rational agency, which in itself seeks a self-interpretation that will constitute a genuine self-understanding once you enact it. Recognizing you as a rational agent therefore entails recognizing you, to that extent, as interested in enacting a character that is true to yourself.

Finally, I must regard you as mirroring all of these realizations with respect to me. I must recognize that you interpret me partly by trying to figure out my self-understanding, and that you take my rational agency to militate against self-misunderstanding on my part as well.

Considering only our rational agency, then, and leaving aside any rationally contingent motives, I will see the two of us as motivated toward an improvisational collaboration not unlike that of theatrical improvisers – a collaboration in which each of us is acting on a shared understanding of what both of us are doing. You will try to act on an accurate interpretation of what you are doing; I will try to act on an accurate interpretation of what I am doing; and each of us will try to interpret the other, partly by sussing out the other's self-understanding. If both of us succeed in all of these endeavors, we'll be on the same page, so to speak, enacting and interpreting us as enacting a single pair of *dramatis personae*.

* * *

For all I have said thus far, however, this improvisational collaboration is not a goal for either of us individually. Each

the term carries normative connotations that may not be appropriate in all cases. For this reason, we tend to reserve the term for cases in which the false self-conception is adopted self-deceptively, in order to avoid some unpleasant truth about oneself.

of us aims for a correct interpretation of both parties, which will be the same interpretation if both of us succeed; but for all I have said thus far, neither of us aims at joint success per se. So although we have individual aims whose simultaneous attainment will produce convergence, neither of us aims at convergence as such – for all I have said thus far.

Yet the realization that such convergence would result from our reaching our individual aims suggests the possibility of adopting convergence as an aim as well. Does rational agency favor adopting that aim? Specifically, does the motive that each of us has for making himself understood to himself also favor making himself understood to the other? In order to answer this question, we must consider a further consequence of the differences between self-enacting improvisation and other improvisational genres.

If you and I were improvising a skit in front of an audience, and if we were especially nimble improvisers, we might try to fascinate our audience by playing deeply conflicted characters in a convoluted plot, full of subterfuge, misunderstandings, and sudden reversals. We would consider ourselves successful if members of the audience were still scratching their heads as they filed out of the theater, debating who did what to whom, and why.

In one sense, the audience might eventually arrive at a full understanding of our performance, just as it could fully understand a drama about straightforward dealings between uncomplicated characters. Yet understanding either performance would entail finding the clearest interpretation of what had transpired onstage, subsuming the dramatic action under the simplest and most coherent set of explanatory hypotheses; and the clearest explanation of the one performance would be less simple and less coherent than the clearest explanation of the other. In that sense, the audience could never understand our convoluted drama as well as it understood one that was more straightforward.

The fundamental form of understanding is generalization. To *com-prehend* something is literally to "grasp together" its particulars under synoptic patterns or principles. Conversely, what the faculty of understanding abhors is the proliferation of principles, or their being larded with exceptions, conditions, and qualifications, which compromise their utility for "grasping together" disparate particulars. If a character's acts and utterances can be grasped, for example, under the pattern of promoting a single, ultimate goal in light of coherent beliefs, then they will be readily comprehensible. The more tangled the web of explanatory patterns becomes, the less comprehension it provides; the simpler an explanation, the greater the resulting comprehension.

To be sure, simplicity is only one of several competing desiderata in an explanation. The best explanation of a phenomenon combines simplicity with empirical adequacy (describing the phenomenon correctly), fruitfulness (explaining as many phenomena as possible), and theoretical unity (cohering with explanations of other phenomena), as well as other virtues. Usually, we must accept trade-offs among these desiderata, since achieving greater empirical adequacy or fruitfulness requires a sacrifice in simplicity, and vice versa. With respect to a given phenomenon, then, the best explanation is not necessarily the simplest.

But when we compare different phenomena, we can see that equally adequate and fruitful explanations of them may differ in simplicity. A phenomenon that can be explained adequately and fruitfully with no sacrifice of simplicity is more comprehensible than one for which an adequate and fruitful explanation must be complex.

That's why the audience would not understand our convoluted performance as well as they would understand one in which the characters knew what they wanted, said what they thought, and did as they said. The audience could understand the performances equally well in the sense of finding the best explanation of either one; but the best explanation of the former would entail greater compromises in the explanatory virtues, thus providing less comprehension. The latter performance, being susceptible to a simpler interpretation, would be more intelligible, though perhaps less entertaining.

✶   ✶   ✶

In self-enactment, however, entertainment is not on the agenda: the point is to understand ourselves, not to have our brains teased in the process. And the question, to repeat, is whether the drive toward understanding ourselves gives each of us a motive for making himself understood to the other.[3]

Just as I can have motives for self-deception, I can have motives for deceiving you about myself. But as in the case of motives for self-deception, any motives for deceiving you would be rationally contingent, incidental to my rational agency. In my capacity as rational agent, I prefer to avoid keeping two sets of books about myself, as would become necessary if I had one interpretation intended for your consumption and another for my own.

Moreover, your actual understanding of me may be relevant to my understanding of you. Insofar as your behavior is directed at me, I have to know what you think I am doing, or am likely to do, in order to understand what you are doing in response or

---

[3] This question is the main concern of Adam Morton's book *The Importance of Being Understood: Folk Psychology as Ethics* (New York: Routledge, 2003). Morton works with the standard consequentialist conception of practical reasoning, and so his version of the question concerns the instrumental advantages of making oneself understood. His answer is that "[w]hen you make yourself intelligible you gain a predictive hold over the behavior of others" (p. vi). Because I work with a different conception of practical reasoning, I arrive at a different answer. My answer, roughly, is that when you make yourself intelligible to others, you improve your chances of continuing to interact with them in ways that are intelligible to you, such intelligibility being the aim that constitutes your rational agency.

anticipation. And this understanding of your behavior may in turn be essential to figuring out how it makes sense for me to go on, since I would have trouble improvising an intelligible rejoinder to behavior of yours that I found unintelligible. Rationally contingent motives aside, I prefer that your behavior be premised on the same understanding of me that I have, so that I can find an intelligible course through our interaction without the need for double bookkeeping.

These considerations can be summed up by means of a contrast between two epistemic extremes. At one extreme, I have a way of interpreting myself, a way that I want you to interpret me, a way that I think you do interpret me, a way that I think you suspect me of wanting you to interpret me, a way that I think you suspect me of thinking you do interpret me, and so on, each of these interpretations being distinct from all the others, and all of them being somehow crammed into my self-conception. At the other extreme, there is just one interpretation of me, which is common property between us,[4] in that we not only hold it but interpret one another as holding it, and so on. If my goal is understanding, then the latter interpretation is clearly preferable, because it is so much simpler while being equally adequate, fruitful, and so on.[5]

To be sure, the latter is not a preferable interpretation of the same phenomena as the former; it's an interpretation of different phenomena, which lend themselves to a simpler but equally adequate and fruitful interpretation. But my reasoning becomes practical precisely when I seek to understand myself by making myself understandable – by becoming a more understandable phenomenon – and I am a more understandable phenomenon when I lend myself to a more coherent and

---

[4] I don't say that these interpretations constitute common *knowledge*, because I make no assumption as to whether they are appropriately justified.

[5] Adam Morton cites "complexity considerations" of this kind in *The Importance of Being Understood*, 18 and 141 ff.

perspicuous interpretation. My drive toward self-understanding
favors making myself amenable to an interpretation that won't
ramify exponentially as I come into contact with others.

Naturally, I hope that you will likewise be interested in converging with me on a shared interpretation of yourself. Insofar
as I regard the two of us merely as rational agents, then, I have
an ideal of improvisational collaboration between us, in which
we enact a shared interpretation of who we are. To repeat, I
may have rationally contingent motives for defecting from this
collaboration in various ways, but rationality itself militates in
favor of it. And in recognizing you as a rational agent, I must
recognize that you have the same rational ideal, though you too
may have contingent motives to the contrary as well. How we
resolve the conflict between these motives is a topic to which I
will return later.

These consequences of agency, as I conceive it, are confirmed by
social-scientific research into a phenomenon that the psycholo-
gist William Swann calls "identity negotiation." Identity negotiation encompasses several processes by which members of a pair or
a group tacitly agree upon a set of roles for each of them to play.

Swann has shown that people tend to gravitate toward others
who view them as they view themselves: they try to change the
minds of others who view them differently; if they fail, they tend
to be dissatisfied in the relationship, even to the point of termi-
nating it; *and these tendencies hold even for people who have negative
views of themselves.*[6] That is, people with negative self-conceptions

---

[6] The research discussed in this paragraph is summarized in William
B. Swann, Jr., "The Self and Identity Negotiation," *Interaction Studies* 6
(2005): 69–83. See also Swann's book *Resilient Identities: Self, Relationships,
and the Construction of Social Reality* (New York: Basic Books, 1999). In
The Presentation of Self in Everyday Life (New York: Anchor Books, 1959),

gravitate toward others who view them negatively; they try to disabuse others of more positive views about them; and they exit relationships with people who persist in viewing them positively. Those with low self-esteem are happier and more likely to remain with roommates or spouses or employers whose opinion of them is as low as their own than with those whose opinion of them is higher.

Identity negotiation also involves processes by which people's images of another person influence him to behave accordingly.[7] When people are given a random description of someone before meeting him for the first time – when they are told, for example, that he is sociable, or that he is belligerent – they proceed to treat him in ways that elicit behavior confirming the description, as judged by independent observers. If before meeting me for the first time, you are told that I am belligerent, then you will behave in ways that induce me to be belligerent, even in the eyes of someone observing me without knowing what you were told. I may even carry the corresponding behavior into subsequent interactions with other people, perhaps because I have applied the description to myself on the basis of the initial interaction. Your having been told that I am belligerent will thus have led you to make me behave belligerently not only with you but also with the next person I meet.[8]

Goffman tends to assume that a social performer will seek to project a positive image of himself. The reason, I suspect, is that Goffman focuses on the strategic goals of the performance, without considering its purely cognitive purpose.

7 The research discussed in this paragraph is summarized in Mark Snyder and Oliver Klein, "Construing and Constructing Others: On the Reality and the Generality of the Behavioral Confirmation Scenario," *Interaction Studies* 6 (2005): 53–67. Some of this research is also discussed in Swann's *Resilient Identities*.

8 If the way I am described to you conflicts with my antecedent self-conception, there may be a "battle of wills," in which I either conform to the description or try to disconfirm it, depending on our relative status and relative degrees of confidence in our conceptions of me. A person of low social status and low confidence in his self-conception may end up internalizing

By means of interpersonal processes such as these, members of a group negotiate agreed-upon roles for each member of the group to play; and if negotiations fail, the group becomes unstable and more likely to disband. The results of these negotiations can look irrational from the perspective of self-interest. Why would anyone give others grounds for thinking ill of him, leave an employer who raises his pay, or induce an interlocutor to be belligerent? Swann's answer is this:[9]

> [P]eople form self-views as a means of making sense of the world, predicting the responses of others, and guiding behavior. From this vantage point, self-views represent the "lens" through which people perceive their worlds and organize their behavior. As such, it is critical that these "lenses" remain stable.

In other words, the obvious costs incurred in identity negotiation are outweighed by cognitive gains in "making sense of the world." In my view, these cognitive gains serve an interest that is not rationally contingent but rather constitutive of rational agency. Hence the self-defeating gambits of identity negotiators are rational at a level deeper than self-interest, which is rational only insofar as it makes us intelligible.[10]

The foregoing considerations do not imply that rationality requires you to be brutally frank. One of your stronger motives

---

the conception that other people have of him, adopting it and acting so as to confirm it. A person of high status and high confidence will act so as to win others over to his conception of himself. And in either case, a failure to reach agreement with others about how to view him will make him uncomfortable and more likely to terminate relations with them.

9 *Resilient Identities,* 70.

10 I expand on this point in Lecture 5. I have defended it in "The Story of Rational Action," *Philosophical Topics* 21 (1993): 229–53; reprinted in *The Possibility of Practical Reason* (Oxford: Oxford University Press, 2000), 144–69.

may be a desire for social harmony, which you can best promote in some circumstances by assuming an amiable expression and keeping your true sentiments to yourself. In those circumstances, putting on an amiable expression makes more sense than baring your soul.

A pretense of this kind is not usually designed to deceive, however.[11] On the contrary, your social face is meant to be seen for what it is, a mask adopted in order to promote social harmony. This mask provides you and others with a shared basis for understanding your behavior, on two levels. On the surface, you proceed to act in ways that would make sense in light of the amiable attitudes that your face pretends to express, and others pretend to understand your actions in terms of those attitudes. At a deeper level, all parties understand the surface performance as a pretense motivated by a desire for social harmony.

You don't entirely avoid the costs of double bookkeeping in this case, since you still have undisclosed attitudes in addition to the socially emollient attitudes that you express. But the former attitudes are irrelevant to your current behavior, and the latter belong to a boilerplate identity that everyone affects in such situations, so that it repays the costs of its complexity in explanatory fruitfulness.

Note that the difference between surface and depth in this case is not that only one level involves a performance; the difference is rather that only one of the performances is authentic. The surface performance is a play within another play, because the underlying role of socially minded pretender is also performed, with an eye to providing a shared basis for understanding your behavior. You authentically play the part of someone

[11] See Thomas Nagel, "Concealment and Exposure," *Philosophy and Public Affairs* 27 (1998): 3–30; reprinted in *Concealment and Exposure* (New York: Oxford University Press, 2002), 3–26. See also my paper "The Genesis of Shame," *Philosophy and Public Affairs* 30 (2001): 27–52, reprinted in *Self to Self* (New York: Cambridge University Press, 2006), 45–69.

pretending to be amiable, on the assumption that others will authentically play the part of pretending to interpret your behavior as amiable, with the result that everyone understands the interaction alike.[12]

Roles or identities are not the only dramatic elements on which self-improvisers are likely to seek agreement; we also seek agreement on scenarios for various kinds of interaction, specifying how those interactions are carried out. Roger Schank and Robert Abelson have argued that a robot would need to know many such scenarios in order to simulate an intelligent agent.[13]

---

[12] Goffman: "We tend to see real performances as something not purposely put together at all, being an unintentional product of the individual's unselfconscious response to the facts of his situation. And contrived performances we tend to see as something painstakingly pasted together, one false item on another, since there is no reality to which the items of behavior could be a direct response. It will be necessary to see now that these dichotomous conceptions are by way of being the ideology of honest performers, providing strength to the show they put on, but a poor analysis of it" (*The Presentation of Self*, 70). "[W]hen we observe a middle-class girl playing dumb for the benefit of her boy friend, we are ready to point to items of guile and contrivance in her behavior. But like herself and her boy friend, we accept as an unperformed fact that this performer *is* a young American middle-class girl. But surely here we neglect the greater part of the performance" (pp. 74–5).

[13] R. C. Schank and R. P Abelson, *Scripts, Plans, Goals, and Understanding: An Inquiry into Human Knowledge Structures* (Hillsdale, NJ: Lawrence Erlbaum Associates, 1977). Schank and Abelson use the term 'script', which strikes my ear as implying that actions and utterances are mandated with more specificity than Schank and Abelson actually have in mind. I prefer the term 'scenario', which suggests a greater degree of indeterminacy, leaving room for improvisation. 'Scenario' is the term that was used for the standard plot outlines on which performers improvised in the commedia dell'arte tradition, and it was adopted by some of the originators of Chicago "improv" theater. (See R. Keith Sawyer, *Improvised Dialogues: Emergence and*

Schank and Abelson's favorite example is the restaurant scenario, which can be pictured as a tree diagram of how a visit to a restaurant typically unfolds. Either you wait to be seated – in which case, you may or may not be asked whether you have a reservation – or you are permitted to seat yourself; then you wait until someone brings a menu or tells you what's available, or both; then you and your companions take turns telling that person your choices from the available items, leaving out condiments, which are already on the table, and dessert, which is ordered later; and so on. Even if you knew that restaurants are places to eat, you would have trouble extracting a meal from one of them if you didn't know how the scenario goes. If you didn't know the scenario, of course, you might ask for directions at the door; but you would then have to know the "asking for directions" scenario.

There was a time when philosophers of action, under the influence of Wittgenstein,[14] believed that actions are explained by being redescribed in a way that places them in a larger pattern. Consider A. I. Melden's example of a driver who

---

Creativity in Conversation [Westport, CT: Ablex Publishing, 2003], 20 ff.) Where Schank and Abelson speak of scripts, and I speak of scenarios, Goffman speaks of "routines" (*The Presentation of Self*, 16 *et passim*). Sawyer discusses the variable specificity of scripts, scenarios, and routines in his *Creating Conversations: Improvisation in Everyday Discourse* (Cresskill, NJ: Hampton Press, 2001). For a recent philosophical discussion of scripts, see Christina Bicchieri, *The Grammar of Society: The Nature and Dynamics of Social Norms* (New York: Cambridge University Press, 2006), 93 ff.

[14] The most relevant passage in Wittgenstein, quoted by Melden, is this:

"I am not ashamed of what I did then, but of the intention which I had." And didn't the intention reside *also* in what I did? What justifies the shame? The whole history of the incident. (*Philosophical Investigations* §644)

explains why he has raised his arm by declaring the intention of signaling a turn:

> [I]n stating his intention in raising his arm, the person is explaining what he is doing. But what he is doing has to be understood as referring not to the present moment, sliced off so to speak from what has gone before and what will follow, but to the present action as an incident in the total proceedings: the driver is on the road, has arrived at an intersection, is about to turn, and is indicating that he is preparing to do so. In declaring his intention in raising his arm, the driver is explaining what he is doing and he is explaining what he is doing, *i.e.* that he is signaling, by directing attention to the context in which the raising of his arm is understood as signaling.[15]

> [T]he statement of motive or intention enables us to make sense of what was going on – it reveals an order or pattern in the proceedings which had not been apparent to the person who asked, 'Why are you ... ?'[16]

Responding to this passage, Donald Davidson argued that talk of "an order or pattern in the proceedings" was empty without some specification of what that pattern might be and why it might be explanatory. Davidson thought that, in the case just cited, the conventional patterns of behavior would not be adequate:

> What is the pattern that explains the action? Is it the familiar pattern of an action done for a reason? Then it does indeed explain the action, but only because it assumes the relation of reason and action that we want to analyze. Or is the pattern rather this: the man is driving, he is approaching a turn; he knows he ought to signal; he knows how to signal, by raising his arm. And now, in this context, he raises his arm. Perhaps ... if all this happens, he does signal. And the explanation would then be this: if, under these conditions, a man raises his arm, then he signals. The difficulty is, of course, that this explanation does not touch the question of

---

[15] A. I. Melden, *Free Action* (London: Routledge and Kegan Paul, 1961), 98–9.
[16] Ibid., 102.

why he raised his arm. He had a reason to raise his arm, but this has not been shown to be the reason why he did it.[17]

In Davidson's view, a reason *for* the driver to raise his arm – consisting in his desire to signal plus his knowledge how to signal – is not displayed as the reason *for which* he raised his arm unless it is asserted to have caused his arm-raising. The reason for him to raise his arm becomes the reason for which he raised it only if it caused that behavior. Hence merely fitting the arm-raising into a "pattern" is not sufficient to explain it, unless the pattern in question is the pattern of cause and effect.

I think that Davidson's causal view is correct, but I also think that in adopting it, subsequent philosophers of action have lost sight of an important element of the Wittgensteinian view. Knowing how to signal a turn is not like knowing how to climb a tree or open a cocoanut: it's not a piece of purely instrumental knowledge. It is knowledge of a move in a conventional scenario shared among drivers. And such scenarios make an independent contribution to our understanding of actions, over and above indicating the causally operative motives. For they are patterns of behavior that we jointly converge on enacting, so that we can understand one another and ourselves as enacting them. A driver may want to take a turn without being hit by other cars, but his desire doesn't simply cause a bodily movement that he personally believes conducive to a collision-free turn. He manifests his desire to turn by enacting part of a scenario conventional among drivers, so that they will understand his movement as the signaling of a turn, so that he can interpret their movements as reactions to such a signal, and he can then see clearly how it makes sense to proceed. To overlook the scenario within which drivers collaboratively improvise their travels is indeed to miss a pattern within which driving behavior must be understood.

[17] "Actions, Reasons and Causes," in *Essays on Actions and Events* (New York: Oxford University Press, 2001), 3–20, p. 11.

The scenario doesn't supersede the ordinary psychological factors in explaining the agents' behavior; indeed, it incorporates them. It is implicit in the scenario that the driver wants to make a turn, and that his desire partly causes his movement. That's how the agreed-upon story goes: the driver wants to turn and is thereby moved to raise his arm as a signal. The scenario is built up out of moves described in terms of their motivational explanations – described, that is, as an attempt to do this or a step directed toward that. Also implicit in the scenario, however, is that the driver manifests his motives in accordance with this very scenario, by which he and others can understand what he's doing, so that they can continue elaborating their joint improvisation in directions intelligible to one another and themselves. Implicit in the scenario, in other words, is that its constituent moves manifest the implicitly specified motives in accordance with the scenario itself.

Imagine that you and I are improvisational actors on stage. I open my mouth and utter some words, accompanied by a bodily gesture. You don't yet know what I am doing, and so you don't know what things might make sense for you to do in response. But then you realize: I am holding a stack of thin booklets in my arm and asking you whether you have a reservation. We are in a restaurant, and I am the maitre d': it's the restaurant scenario. And now you know which lines of response would make sense.

When you enter an actual restaurant, of course, you are not as clueless as an improvisational actor on stage, who may not know whether he will be called upon to enact "Dinner at Joe's" or "The Siege of Troy." But small moments of improvisational confusion still occur. As you enter the restaurant and I approach, you may ask yourself, "Is this the maitre d', or is it another patron on his way out?" – which is just to ask, "Are we doing the host-and-guest routine, or the fellow-patron routine?" One scenario calls for you to address me directly; the other calls for you to smile and step to one side.

To say that these scenarios "call for" different responses makes them sound normative, as if they dictate what you ought to do. And of course there is a norm of courtesy dictating that if approached in the entry of a commercial establishment by another customer passing in the opposite direction, you ought to smile and step aside. The responses called for when greeted by the maitre d' of a restaurant are also subject to norms of courtesy: you should not shove your nose into his face and bellow "Food!" In the case of your response to the maitre d', however, the scenario is far more specific than the norms of courtesy. It offers a small selection of particular moves that can propel the action to the next scene, from the entryway to the table. Insofar as the scenario is normative in recommending these moves, its normative force is not that of courtesy but merely that of rationality – which is to say that it is the normative force of what it makes sense to do.

Each of the specified moves makes sense at two levels: first, because its specification alludes to the attitudes or traits that would prompt someone like you to make that move; and, second, because you would prefer that those attitudes and traits prompt a move that is included, along with its motivational explanation, in this very scenario, which embodies common knowledge among the parties as to how the sequel can be developed intelligibly. If the question is "Why did you just tell the waiter, 'I'll have the club sandwich'?," the short answer may be, "Because I want a club sandwich, and that's the way to get one." A longer answer, however, would expand on the phrase 'the way to get one', which says more than that the utterance in question is conducive to securing the desired meal. It says that utterances like this are the way meals are gotten hereabouts, part of the way things are done. Fully expanded, then, the explanation might continue, "Of all the means by which a meal might be extracted from yonder kitchen – and I don't have time to consider them all – this is the one that will be understood by the locals as a move in the restaurant scenario, so that they'll respond in ways that not only tend to fulfill my desire but also make sense to me, so that I'll know what it makes sense for me to do in return, even if they don't quite fulfill my desire (for example, if the kitchen is out of turkey), and we'll jointly manage to improvise our way through to the outcome of my being fed."

Vast stretches of our social life are governed by conventional scenarios of this kind. We are like an improvisational theater troupe that, over many years of performing together, has developed an extensive repertoire of scenes that any member of the troupe can initiate in the expectation that the others will follow suit. Again, we do not face one another on a bare stage, where we must converge on a scenario chosen arbitrarily from our repertoire. We face one another in determinate circumstances, with more or less determinate identities that have been formed in prior negotiations. But even if you are unmistakably my colleague, and you knock on what is unmistakably my office door, a question remains whether you are about to initiate the philosophical-query scenario, the unfinished-committee-business scenario, the invitation-to-lunch scenario, the let's-procrastinate-by-shooting-the-breeze scenario, or even the oops-I-meant-to-knock-on-your-neighbor's-door scenario. In any case, you have already initiated the knock-on-the-door scenario, according to which, after I say "Come in," the next move is yours. I await that move, from which I will then take my cue.[18]

∗   ∗   ∗

The totality of the repertoire shared among us is what might be called our way of life. What I have argued thus far is that rational agency favors participating in a shared way of life, in

[18] For observations on the range of conversational scenarios, see Goffman, "Footing," in *Forms of Talk* (Philadelphia: University of Pennsylvania Press, 1981), 124–59.

order to have access to the resources for self-understanding that it affords. Creatures improvising behavior intelligible to themselves are under pressure to develop a way of life, and this pressure emanates from that which makes them rational agents.

A solitary rational agent would be under similar pressure, even if he never interacted with other agents. For he would face repeatable situations, in which the things that he could intelligibly do, and their ranking as more or less intelligible, would yield general knowledge of what would make sense in any relevantly similar situation. He would therefore develop a way of doing things, which would then become self-reinforcing, because doing things that way would begin to make sense, not only for the reasons that initially made it intelligible, but also for the additional reason that he has developed standing knowledge of its intelligibility, which has entrenched it in his way of life.

If two such solitary agents came into contact with one another, they would begin figuring out one another's way of life. Figuring out one another's way of life would entail not only noting one another's ways of doing things but also interpreting one another's modes of self-understanding. One of these agents might then adopt the other's way of doing something because it is instrumentally superior: maybe the other has invented a better gizmo for trapping mice. The first agent might also borrow elements from the other's way of life on independent, cognitive grounds, as a better way of making sense to himself: maybe the other has found a more coherent way of incorporating conflicting needs into a single life.

And then there would also be convergence for the sake of social self-understanding. When an agent figures out how the other understands himself, he will learn categories under which he can be fairly confident of making himself understood to the other; and he will then see that by doing things whose interpretation by the other he can anticipate, he will be better prepared to understand the other's reaction, so as to figure out an intelligible way of dealing with it.[19] Doing something whose interpretation by the other he could not anticipate would be more likely to elicit a baffling response, from which he couldn't tell how it made sense to go on. Each agent therefore has a cognitive incentive to act under explanatory concepts held by the other, so as to raise his chances of having access to a range of intelligible options when his next turn comes around. And of course the chances of making sense throughout extended interactions will be raised by a repertoire of action concepts chained together in shared scenarios. The two previously solitary agents will thus be pressed to develop a shared way of life, though each may retain some private lifeways as well.

The importance of participating in socially shared scenarios should not be underestimated. If upon entering a restaurant you departed too far from the relevant scenario, you would become a kind of social outlaw, and like an outlaw you would find yourself in a no-man's-land where others would have to take unorthodox measures to deal with you, leaving you no clearly intelligible avenues of response.

Think of those stories in which the protagonist gets himself further and further committed to some outrageous deception. These stories owe their dramatic tension to the increasing unpredictability of the protagonist's actions, both for the audience and for the protagonist himself. He asks aloud, "*Now what am I going to do?*," and the audience shares his puzzlement: What *is* he going to do next? The puzzle is not that there is no way of going on; it's almost that there are too many. Having departed so far from the way things are done – told such outlandish lies, stolen such absurd sums, or whatever – he is now in a trackless territory where he might do or say just about

---

[19] Goffman: "[I]n learning to perform our parts in real life we guide our own productions by not too consciously maintaining an incipient familiarity with the routine of those to whom we will address ourselves" (*The Presentation of Self*, 72).

anything, though just about anything he did would be surprising or bizarre. He is improvising without a scenario, beyond the limits of any known repertoire. The protagonist usually displays his endearing genius by finding *something to do next*, something that makes sense as the next step down the chartless course that he has taken. Few of us nonfictional characters are blessed with that endearing genius.

If you replace my phrase 'way of life' with 'form of life', and my term 'scenario' with 'practice', you will now see even greater similarities between my philosophy of action and the one attributed earlier to followers of Wittgenstein. Much of what we do, according to my view, is not just a matter of moving our bodies so as to satisfy our desires in light of our beliefs; it is a matter of manifesting such motives, of course, but of doing so in the enactment of action concepts contextually defined by their place in socially shared practices. To order a meal is not merely to emit sounds privately believed conducive to the desired outcome of receiving food; it is to enact part of a practice, motivated indeed by the desire for food, but also guided, first, by the concept 'ordering a meal', which renders the move intelligible in terms of such a desire to those conversant with the practice, and second, by the need to do something intelligible in such socially recognized terms, so as to facilitate ongoing intelligibility in the interaction.

We are thus dependent on socially developed practices for the realization of our rational autonomy, at least when interacting with others.[20] Our individual practical reasoning, plus the necessity of interacting with other practical reasoners, gives us an incentive to converge with them on a shared practical

---

[20] See Alasdair MacIntyre, "The Intelligibility of Action," in *Rationality, Relativism and the Human Sciences,* ed. J. Margolis, M. Krausz, and R. M. Burian (Dordrecht: Martinus Nijhoff, 1986), 63–80.

vocabulary in which we can understand one another. Without such a shared vocabulary, we would struggle to find understandable ways of responding to others who haven't made themselves understood to us, partly because we never made ourselves understood to them, in the first place. We escape from this Babel by developing a common pool of situationally defined action concepts, and by drawing on this pool for our ideas of intelligible things to do. We then come to depend on socially shared resources for realizing our rational autonomy.

Practical reason exerts an influence not just on single decisions but over the long run, as it guides the gradual development and modification of our shared way of life. With respect to this phenomenon, however, my explanation shows less resemblance to Wittgenstein than to Kant.

A true Wittgensteinian would say that the reasoning by which we figure out how to modify our practices is itself a practice, also subject to modification by a practice, and so on indefinitely, with nothing but *practices all the way down*. In my view, however, we have practices at all partly because of needing to make sense to ourselves while living with others who have the same need, and the criterion of success for modifying our practices is whether we thereby manage to make more sense – that is, whether the resulting way of life is more intelligible and better enables us to find intelligible courses of action. Judging the rationality of socially developed practices is not just another socially developed practice, because it rests on an objective criterion set by the aim that's constitutive of agency and practical reason.

Let us consider, then, how one way of life might make more or less sense than another. How can we jointly refine our repertoire of scenarios so as to improve our intelligibility to ourselves?

Here is one example. It is a common observation that over the course of history, societies have tended to dispense with various distinctions among persons, where they have proved dispensable, and that this tendency represents a form of social progress. We find that we no longer need distinct versions of our situational scenarios for cases in which the participants are of different genders, races, castes, or nationalities. We can treat a conversation merely as a conversation, whether the company be male, female, or mixed; we can treat a sale merely as a sale, a meal merely as a meal, a gift merely as a gift, whatever the races or economic classes of the participants.

I want to say that the tendency to dispense with dispensable distinctions in the design of our socially shared scenarios represents progress that is specifically rational – progress according to the objective standard set by the constitutive aim of agency, the standard of intelligibility. As I pointed out earlier, the fundamental form of understanding is generalization, the "grasping together" of disparate particulars under general principles, whose utility for comprehension is compromised when they are multiplied, or larded with exceptions, qualifications, and special conditions. To compound our situational scenarios by the roles of gender, race, and caste is to multiply principles, or stuff them with conditions, in just this way, yielding a way of life that is less comprehensible, less readily grasped together. To eliminate social distinctions where possible usually results in a more comprehensible way of life.

The rational pressure to dispense with distinctions in our socially shared scenarios will be reinforced by the need to coordinate those distinctions with our values. We can make sense of ourselves as characters in the standard scenarios only insofar as we actually have the motives that the scenarios call upon us to enact. And as I explained in Lecture 2, we seek intelligibility in our motives by directing them by and large toward recognizable

kinds of things, and toward the same kinds of things as other
people, so as to minimize our need to make explanatory exceptions.[21] Each person is under some degree of rational pressure
to cultivate responses that can be "grasped together" with his
other responses and the responses of others, and this pressure will reinforce, and be reinforced by, the tendency toward
scenarios in which everyone can play. To put it the other way
around, if our scenarios call for different behavior in a given
role from players of different genders or races, then we will succeed in making sense to ourselves by enacting those scenarios
only if our motives differ accordingly, and hence only insofar
as we have failed to converge on shared values. Conversely, the
pressure to converge on shared values may favor gender- and
race-neutral scenarios as well.

I have spoken of a tendency to dispense with distinctions among
the players in situational scenarios where such distinctions are
dispensable. How do we tell whether we can dispense with a
distinction?

The answer is that some revisions in our way of life would leave
us with scenarios that we cannot enact, or cannot enact authentically. For example, there are some adult roles that children and
adolescents are simply not competent to play. We therefore find
that we cannot dispense with some distinctions of age. There
may be some gender-neutral roles that both men and women
can play, but not authentically. Enacting these roles, many men
or women may find themselves falsifying their motives or convictions or emotions. When they try to change the way they think
and feel, so as better to inhabit gender-neutral roles, they may

---

[21] Of course, we direct our motives in this way only insofar as it's possible and
   intelligible for us to do so, given our understandable interest in preserving
   our individuality.

find their efforts unsuccessful; they may even fail in their efforts to raise children who can inhabit these roles with authenticity. If so – and I'm not saying that it is so, only that it may be – then we will have found that some distinctions of gender are indispensable, that gender is not an epicycle in our way of life but an ineliminable category, because we cannot make good, honest sense to ourselves without it.

In making rational progress of this kind, practical reasoning is an experimental discipline. Often we don't know in advance whether we can authentically enact a way of life that differs in some respects from our own; we don't know in advance whether one change in our way of life would eventually oblige us to make others, or whether we would still find ourselves with a clearer, more coherent self-understanding once the ensuing cascade of changes came to rest. We don't know, that is, until we try. Figuring out how to live is a process of trial and error, in which the trials are what Mill called experiments in living.[22] Mill's case for the liberty to carry out such experiments gains support from the very nature of practical reasoning, as I conceive it. When we are prevented from making experiments in living, we are prevented from figuring out how to live, because the way to live is the way that would make us most intelligible to ourselves, which cannot be deduced a priori.

Modifying our way of life also involves two distinct phases of practical reasoning, as in the case of modifying our individual characters, which I discussed in Lecture 1.[23] In order to arrive at a way of life in which we will be more intelligible to ourselves, we may have to take practical steps of social or self-reform, which must in turn be understood in the context of the life that we already have. Ideally, we will discover understandable steps by which to arrive at a more understandable way of life. But we may also have to strike compromises between these two phases of

[22] "On Liberty" (New York: Barnes and Noble Books, 2004), 59.
[23] See p. 24.

self-understanding. In extreme cases, our existing way of life
may afford no intelligible way of implementing reforms that
would clearly make it more intelligible.

Note, then, that the very brief considerations that I have
adduced for the rationality of dispensing with social distinctions
are not intended as an a priori demonstration that doing so is
rationally required everywhere and always. Whether it is rational in a given case depends on whether it can be accomplished
intelligibly and whether it makes our way of life more intelligible, which must be discovered experimentally. All I claim is
that we should expect a tendency, overall and in the long run,
for distinctions to be minimized, insofar as we can authentically
conduct our lives with a less complex set of social roles.

The gradual, cumulative form of this process allows relatively
weak elements in our nature to have an eventual impact, if they
are sufficiently persistent. An example is the rational pressure
against deception, which I discussed earlier.

This pressure is too weak to outweigh our specific motives for
deception on some occasions. The costs of deception in terms
of finding an intelligible course through an interaction may
simply be outweighed by the benefits peculiar to the interaction itself. Lying sometimes pays. Yet the costs are sufficiently
systematic to generate conflicts on many occasions, frequently
complicating the question of what it would make sense for us to
do. When the rational motive against deception is clearly the
weaker motive, we would not understand ourselves better by acting on it, but we might well understand ourselves better on other
occasions – and, indeed, overall – if the incentives to deception
were removed and, with them, the systematic costs of the resulting conflict.

The cognitive economy of self-understanding may therefore
favor developing values and scenarios that are compatible with

this relatively weak but persistent element in our rational nature. It needn't dominate our motivation or self-understanding on any particular occasion in order to affect which way of life would make us most intelligible to ourselves.

I have gradually enlarged my focus from two self-enacting improvisers, you and me, to the large and lasting company of improvisers to which we belong. Let me narrow the focus again, in order to summarize what has emerged in response to my opening question: How should I regard you upon recognizing your rational agency?

Even if I agree with you about the role that you are improvising, I can still have attitudes toward two different aspects of you. I can have attitudes toward you either under the guise of the role or under the guise of a self-enacting improviser – toward you as the character you are playing, or toward you as the player.

When I interact with you, I interact, in the first instance, with a character, who has many attitudes and traits that I take you to be both manifesting and enacting.[24] These attitudes and traits partly determine how you will respond to my behavior, thus partly determining how it makes sense for me to behave. In anticipating your response, however, I should not think of myself as eliciting it directly and solely from your characteristics. Your response will be determined also by your perception of how it would be intelligible for you to manifest those characteristics in responding.

Thus, I should not think of myself as simply probing your convictions, tempting your appetites, or inflaming your temper; I am extending the jointly improvised scenario with actions

---

[24] I used these terms in Lecture 1 to distinguish between "manifesting" the brute behavioral disposition that comes with having a motive, on the one hand, and "enacting" one's conception of what makes sense in light of having the motive, on the other.

in response to which you will both manifest and enact those attributes, as seems to you most intelligible in light of them – or perhaps in light of other attributes belonging to a revised self-conception that may now strike you as affording even greater self-understanding. In this respect, my behavior should be addressed to you in both of your capacities, just as the behavior of a theatrical improviser is, on the one hand, a dramatized action addressed by a character to the other characters and, on the other, an addition to the collaborative work in progress, addressed by a player to the other players.

The attitude outlined here has a moral coloration – to my eye, at least. It appears to be tinged with shades of reciprocity or respect.

What lends the attitude its moral coloration, I think, is the recognition that no matter what occasion-specific transaction you and I may enter into, there will always be an additional, generic transaction on which it rides. Whether we interact as lender and borrower, questioner and respondent, promisor and promisee, confider and confidant, or whatever, we will also be interacting as self-enacting improvisers each of whom seeks to proceed through the transaction in a way that makes sense for him. The surface transaction may place our characters in positions of inequality or conflict, but the underlying encounter between us as players puts us on an equal footing and obliges us to collaborate. In order to steer an intelligible course through the surface transaction, I need to understand what course you are taking, which must be understood in light of how you understand the course I am taking, and so on – all of which will be difficult to understand if these multiple interpretations are at odds. As participants in the improvisation, then, and apart from any occasion-specific motives we may have for deception, we have a shared interest in establishing a shared understanding of who we are and what we are doing. Even when playing characters who are unequal or mutually hostile, we have a common interest in having them join in a single drama, based on a common understanding of the action onstage.

In pursuit of this common interest, we generally rely on one another's knowledge of a shared repertoire of scenarios, most of which are common property among a larger company of improvisers. You and I can adapt these scenarios to our own immediate purposes, and our adaptations may potentially constitute a tiny contribution to the socially shared repertoire. What we generally cannot do, however, is to strike out entirely on our own, improvising without any shared scenario at all.

While seeing one another as collaborators, then, we also see ourselves as jointly belonging to a larger collaboration. In order to *get on* individually, we have to *get along* with one another, which really does entail *going along* to some extent with behavioral schemas that aren't our invention or property. Each of us realizes his own rational autonomy in concert with the other, by drawing jointly on socially shared resources for self-understanding.

One final note. Virtually all of the considerations adduced in this lecture could in principle be accommodated by a standard account of rationality as a matter of maximizing expected utility. All that would be needed is the additional assumption that we attach utility to self-understanding. But our attaching utility to self-understanding would then be conceived as a rationally contingent preference, and the consequences that I have outlined would amount to rational progress only in relation to that preference, hence only contingently.

My view, by contrast, is that the aim of self-understanding is constitutive of rational agency, and that the consequences outlined here are therefore objectively rational, in the sense that they represent progress in relation to an aim that is inescapable for rational agents. Lecture 5 will be devoted to considering what sort of objectivity that is.

4

Reflecting

I arrived at my conception of agency by squeezing the duplicity, or doubleness, out of an imagined improvisational actor. To begin with, I imagined away the distinction between the player and the character he plays, by imagining that he plays his actual self. Then I imagined away the distinction between the player and his audience, by imagining that his performance is addressed, in the first instance, to himself. I noted that the actor playing to himself can accommodate his audience by doing what it is already prepared to understand; that the audience can rely on the actor to be thus accommodating; but that they need to acknowledge their collaboration, since pretending to work independently will still involve duplicity.

In thinking of rational agency as the result of overcoming doubleness, I am following a venerable tradition. Many philosophers have observed that properly functioning agency requires inner fractures to be healed. Plato thought that rational agency requires unification in the form of cooperation between divisions of the soul. Harry Frankfurt thinks it requires identification with parts of oneself – which, after all, is the overcoming of a division between an identifying self and a self identified with.[1] In my

---

[1] For this point, see my "Identification and Identity," in *Contours of Agency: Essays on Themes from Harry Frankfurt,* edited by Sarah Buss and Lee Overton (Cambridge, MA: MIT Press, 2002), 91–123; reprinted in *Self to Self* (New York: Cambridge University Press, 2006), 330–60.

view, an agent properly unified is more like an improvisational actor who is ingenuously and knowingly portraying himself, for himself.

Each conception of agency points to a characteristic pitfall. For Plato, an agent must beware of dissension between the divisions of his soul; for Frankfurt, he is at the additional risk of failing to identify decisively with either of the warring parties, thus falling into ambivalence. But I doubt whether psychic conflict or ambivalence is the pitfall most characteristic of agency. Inner conflict is not peculiar to rational agents: even a dog can be torn between exuberant play and obedience to its master. And although a dog cannot be reflectively ambivalent between these alternatives, as a rational agent can, I think that reflective ambivalence is sometimes a healthy exercise of rational agency, not a failing.[2] What is both peculiar to rational agents and a pitfall for them, I think, is reflective inauthenticity. Only a rational agent can play false with himself; and playing false with himself is the characteristic failure of agency – a failure of the psychological mechanisms by which agency normally works.

What I have called inauthenticity need not involve intentional self-deception. Inauthenticity can result from less-than-intentional dishonesty of a sort that is easy to understand, given the workings of agency.

A rational agent tends to enact the attitudes and traits that he conceives himself to have, by pursuing what he thinks that he wants, through means in which he thinks that he believes, and in ways characteristic of other dispositions that he ascribes to himself.

---

[2] I argued for this claim at the end of Lecture 2. See also my "Identification and Identity"; and Part 3 of "Persons in Prospect," *Philosophy and Public Affairs* 36 (2008): 222–88.

If he doesn't actually have the attitudes or traits that he imagines as favoring such behavior, then he may not get around to undertaking it, or he may not carry it through to completion. But it may be adequately supported instead by motives other than the ones that he takes to be supporting it. For example, he may do something partly out of ambition and partly because it makes sense to him as expressing a self-ascribed public spirit. Or mistaking belligerence for resoluteness, he may carry through actions manifesting the one because they make sense to him as manifesting the other.

The rational agent thus tends to confirm his own misdiagnoses of his motivational state. He can easily take himself to know himself better than he actually does, because he withholds any disconfirming evidence, not with the intention to deceive, but because it would consist in behavior that didn't make sense in light of what he "knows" about himself. He can also mistake the source of his self-knowledge, thinking that such knowledge is easier to attain than it is. What he is doing here and now is usually known to him spontaneously, without observation, because his agency tends to show him only what he already expects. But he can get the impression that the reason why he knows what he's doing is rather that his behavior is transparent to his introspection.

In short, the very processes that facilitate a rational agent's self-knowledge can also lull him into a dangerous complacency about it. What's worse, they tend to encourage wishful thinking. For he no sooner thinks something about himself than it appears to be true.

Now, I have explained how an agent's wishful thinking can be harmless, even constructive, because it yields genuine self-knowledge.[3] By thinking of himself as furious rather than merely irritated, or as awestruck rather than afraid, he can actually shape his attitude and behavior accordingly, so that the self-interpretation sticks. Even interpretations that are initially false

[3] See especially Lecture 2, pp. 29–30.

can become true over time through the habituating effects of the
actions that they render intelligible. Falsely thinking of himself
as public-spirited, the agent may do things that make sense to
him as public-spirited, and he may thereby acquire a public spirit,
thus correcting his false belief, not by revising it, but by making it
come true.[4]

The problem is that these virtuous kinds of wishful thinking
can easily slip into the less-than-virtuous kind. Without intention-
ally trying to exploit the power of wishful thinking, the agent can
fail to distinguish between the cases in which his thoughts will
be self-fulfilling and the cases in which they won't. Accustomed
to thinking ahead of the facts about himself and relying on them
to catch up, he can fail to notice when they are no longer following. He will notice soon enough, of course, if his gross bodily
movements fail to match what he has just anticipated doing. But
at a psychologically rich level of description, he can easily persist in mischaracterizing his behavior, by giving reactions a label
that they have never come to merit, or attributing his behavior to
motives that it never actually manifests. Because he can generally
trust a thought like "I'll open the door" to come true, he starts to
place similar trust in more interpretive self-descriptions, failing
to notice when they don't quite fit the behavior that ensues. He
thinks, "I'll say something supportive," and offers a backhanded
compliment; he thinks, "I'll get down to work by clearing away
these distractions," and then proceeds to procrastinate.

How can a rational agent protect himself against inauthenticity? In order to guard against it, he will need a mode of thought
distinct from the ones implicated in his rational agency. He will

---

4 Social psychologists who study this phenomenon tend to regard it as
irrational. See, e.g., S.J. Sherman, "On the Self-erasing Nature of Errors
of Prediction," *Journal of Personality and Social Psychology* 39 (1980): 211–21.
I regard it as the height of rationality.

need to suspend the self-assurance with which, as audience, he trusts his interpretations to be borne out and with which, as player, he trusts his actions to be understood. He will need to view all of this self-dealing with suspicion. Best of all would be to occupy such a point of view while his self-enactment and self-interpretation are in progress, so that he can look for telltale signs of overacting or runaway wishful thinking.

What the agent needs, in other words, is to watch the performer and audience in himself from the wings, taking a sideways-on perspective uncommitted to the action or the going interpretation of it. From this perspective, he should be able to detect attempts to enact what he cannot be, or to deny that he is not just being but enacting what he is.

Unlike the roles of player and audience, which can be intermingled, the role of backstage onlooker requires a degree of mental compartmentalization, since it requires a skeptical suspension of the very self-interpretation that is being applied and enacted in the other two roles. This role must therefore be carried out in a partially encapsulated mental process, a train of thought selectively insulated from the mental processes involved in self-enactment and first-order self-interpretation. This train of thought contains interpretations of the agent's behavior that will not be enacted and are not meant to be. It is therefore detached from the feedback loop of interpretation and enactment that gives the agent his experience of selfhood in the practical realm. The result is that, from the agent's point of view, this process of self-observation seems to take place in a consciousness that is his own and yet separate, watching from behind the scenes as he plays himself.

I suggest that this compartmentalized train of reflective thought is what we ordinarily call the conscience. And it is the conscience that keeps the rational agent honest, if anything does.

Take the ordinary notion of the conscience as seeing into the inner recesses of the person's heart. At first glance, this notion

can seem to make no sense. Given that the conscience is part
of the person, and that its examination of his heart is therefore
his own self-examination, why don't we say that *he* sees into the
recesses of his heart? The answer, of course, is that his conscience
sees things that even he doesn't admit to himself. So there must
be three different perspectives from which the person deals
with himself: the perspective of the one who doesn't admit these
things, the perspective of the one to whom he doesn't admit
them, and the perspective of the one who sees them nevertheless.
I have simply offered a further characterization of these perspectives and their roles in rational agency: they are the perspectives
of player, audience, and now of conscience. What differentiates
the conscience from the self who doesn't admit things to himself,
and from the self to whom he doesn't admit them, is that the latter two are parties to the collaborative activity of self-addressed
self-presentation, whereas the conscience views their collaboration without participating – or, as I have put it, from backstage.

My account of rational agency suggests that our ordinary talk
of someone's not admitting things to himself, and of his conscience as seeing them, is not a metaphor or a self-dramatizing
fantasy; it's an accurate description of an actual drama, constituted by distinct functions that are psychologically real. If a person were not presenting himself to himself, he would not be an
autonomous agent capable of practical reasoning. The mental
processes that make him an agent also make him susceptible
to inauthenticity, detection of which requires a distinct mental
process, in the form of a conscience.

* * *

We ordinarily think of the conscience as giving rise to the moral
emotions of guilt and shame. How can these emotions be gener-
ated by an observing awareness in the wings?

Well, the sideways-on view from the wings of an agent's self-
enactment takes in his interactions with other agents, and with
respect to these interactions, it can accommodate thoughts that

would distract the agent from his improvisational task. Hence the conscience can reflect on the dynamics among the players, each of whom relies on the others to help him keep the improvisational ball in the air. The conscience is thus aware of the agent's dependence on, and his resulting vulnerability to, those with whom he interacts, who are in a position either to facilitate or to undercut his exercise of his own rational agency.

Awareness of this dependence on others can give rise to anxiety at the prospect of social disqualification.[5] When the agent bungles his self-presentation, for example, he risks being disqualified from joint improvisation on the grounds of being incompetent at self-enactment. Examples of disqualifying faux pas include failures of bodily self-control (belching, flatulence, blushing), failures of dress (showing slips, open flies), and other failures to police the boundaries of privacy. On the basis of such failures, the agent may be deemed unable to sustain a character on the social stage. The same risk arises when an agent is stripped of the power to present himself – say, by being caught in the meshes of a stereotype, or by being pilloried, either literally or figuratively. When someone is stamped with a character that he hasn't fashioned for himself, his only alternatives are to suffer misinterpretation or to play along – to put on blackface, as it were – and in either case he will be revealed as less than fully empowered to enact himself.

Anxiety about social disqualification constitutes the emotion of shame.[6] The subject of shame envisions being unable to

---

[5] On social disqualification, see Thomas Nagel's "Concealment and Exposure," *Philosophy and Public Affairs* 27 (1998): 3–30; reprinted in *Concealment and Exposure* (New York: Oxford University Press, 2002), 3–26.

[6] Here I reprise the analysis of shame in "The Genesis of Shame," *Philosophy and Public Affairs* 30 (2001): 27–52; reprinted in *Self to Self*, 45–69. One might think that some of the cases discussed here involve embarrassment rather than shame. Let me respond by explaining how I distinguish between the two.

Note that 'embarrassment' is not, in the first instance, the name of an emotion at all. The primary meaning of the verb 'to embarrass' is "to impede or encumber," and the noun 'embarrassment' refers to either the

mount a credible performance. Shame may prompt him to contrive an exit, actual or symbolic – say, by hiding his face or hanging his head – so that he can stage a fresh entrance fully in character, hoping now to pull it off.

The anxiety of shame is not felt from the perspective of the conscience; it is felt from the perspective of the agent, who relies on others to acknowledge him as a competent presenter of self. The role of the conscience is to perceive the risk that he is facing onstage, and either to whisper it to him or maybe just to remind him of it by being mutely present in the wings, perceiving it. The self-enacting agent needs only to see the skepticism in the eyes of his conscience – skepticism that is obvious to him,

encumbrance or the state of being encumbered. (Hence the concept of "financial embarrassments," which are not so called because they tend to make one blush.) Insofar as 'embarrassment' refers to a mental state, it refers to the state of being mentally encumbered or impeded – that is, baffled, confounded, or flustered. In this generic sense, embarrassment can be a component or concomitant of any disconcerting emotion, including shame.

In recent times, 'embarrassment' has also come to denote a particular emotion distinct from shame. (This use of the term is little more than a hundred years old, according to the OED.) This emotion begins with the sense of being the focus of undue or unwelcome attention – typically, ridicule or derision – and it culminates in self-consciousness, the self-focussed attention that hinders fluid speech and behavior (and that consequently counts as embarrassment in the generic sense). Being flustered in the face of laughter is the typical case of the emotion called embarrassment. This emotion differs from shame, first, because it involves self-consciousness rather than anxiety and, second, because it involves a sense of attracting unwelcome recognition rather than of losing social recognition altogether. Being ridiculed is an essentially social kind of treatment. Self-consciousness in the face of ridicule is therefore different from anxiety at the prospect of social disqualification. Whereas the subject of embarrassment feels that he has egg on his face, the subject of shame feels a loss of face – the difference being precisely that between presenting a target for ridicule and not presenting a target for social interaction at all.

since he himself is feeling it – and straightaway he adverts to the eyes of others, in which he risks being discredited as a fellow improviser.

*   *   *

Shame is usually thought to be about something untoward in the self, something that the subject is *a*shamed *of.* But I think that the subject of shame needn't be ashamed of anything in particular, and certainly not of something untoward.[7]

This possibility is exemplified by the stocks, to which people were sentenced precisely because they were assumed not to be sufficiently ashamed of their misdeeds. The stocks were designed to shame them by fixing them in a position that would be intrinsically humiliating, independently of any particular flaw or fault of which they might or might not be ashamed. Their position was humiliating because they were publicly displayed but barred from self-display, unable either to hang their heads or to hold them up. Similarly, a person branded with a racial epithet may feel shame without necessarily being ashamed of his race, because the epithet invokes a stereotype that denies him the opportunity to define himself.

Even when shame is induced by a specific feature of the self, that feature needn't be an object of disapproval, and so it needn't be anything to be ashamed of. Being seen naked can be an occasion for shame even for someone who is proud of his body. Similarly, an extraordinarily beautiful person can feel stereotyped by his own beauty, as it were, because he feels that it

---

[7] The distinction that I draw in this section is not the same as the distinction, drawn in Lecture 2, between feeling a response such as shame in a situation and finding it to have a disvalue such as being shameful. Here I argue that one's situation can actually be shameful, and that one can correctly find it shameful, even though one has no particular thing – no flaw or fault or blemish – to be ashamed of.

defines him for others and thereby undermines his efforts at self-presentation. Some people blush when praised, despite being proud of what they are praised for, because they cannot bear to enact their pride and are therefore at a loss for how to act. The praise holds them up to view, helpless to present themselves.

When we describe someone as being *a*shamed *of* something bad about himself, what we really mean is that he tries to keep it private, and that its exposure to public view would therefore constitute a failure of self-presentation, sufficient to occasion shame. If the person didn't try to keep the matter private – if he just humbly confessed it or brazenly flaunted it – we wouldn't say that he was ashamed of it, precisely because its exposure would no longer amount to a failure of privacy. His keeping it under wraps makes it a part of him that could be stripped naked, and that possibility is what makes it a potential occasion for shame.

An agent in shame can usually reestablish his capability for self-enactment fairly quickly, so that he no longer has to worry about being discounted as incompetent. A different worry about social disqualification is not so easily dispelled. When the agent takes unfair advantage of his fellow improvisers, when he fails to reciprocate the collaborative spirit in which they engage with him, he faces the prospect of being regarded as unreliable in joint improvisation – competent onstage but not to be trusted. The anxiety aroused by this prospect is a form of guilt.[8]

---

[8] Here I reprise the analysis of guilt in "Don't Worry, Feel Guilty," *Philosophy and the Emotions*, Royal Institute of Philosophy Supplement 52, ed. Anthony Hatzimoysis (Cambridge: Cambridge University Press, 2003), 235–48; reprinted in *Self to Self*, 156–69. My account of guilt bears similarities to Thomas M. Scanlon's account of blame, which is also based on the notion of a rupture in relationships. See his *Moral Dimensions: Permissibility, Meaning, Blame* (Cambridge, MA: Harvard University Press, 2008), Chapter 4.

Roughly speaking, I conceive of guilt as anxiety about being in an indefensible position that might warrant one's being cut off from social interaction. What's indefensible about one's position need not be that one has done something immoral, since one can feel guilty for having forgotten a birthday or failed to return a phone call. Indeed, the indefensibility of one's position need not involve one's having done anything at all, since one can feel "survivor guilt" about having been spared some catastrophe that has befallen others. One can even feel guilty for receiving an undeserved benefit, such as favoritism at the expense of siblings or coworkers. In all of these cases, one is anxiously aware of having nothing to say for oneself on a matter that could understandably disrupt some personal connection, usually by arousing resentment.

The connection at risk need not be a special relationship; it may simply be a connection to other people in virtue of their willingness to treat one as a co-improviser in social interactions. That connection is threatened when one has violated the spirit or shared understandings of joint improvisation. One may then feel anxious about being liable to exclusion from joint improvisation in the future – about being dropped, shunned, banned, exiled, outlawed, either by particular people or by people in general, if they are no longer willing to let their self-enactments get tangled up with one's own. Insofar as one feels vulnerable to being cut off by particular people for particular purposes – by former friends, say, for the purpose of future friendship – one's anxiety falls short of the guilt that philosophers call moral; insofar as one feels vulnerable to being cut off by fellow improvisers generally, one's anxiety has the character of moral guilt.

As with shame, this form of guilt is not felt from the perspective of the conscience; it's felt by the agent, in the face of a prospect envisioned in response to what the conscience is felt to be seeing. And what the conscience is felt to be seeing is the backstage view of the agent's self-enactment, a view from which inauthenticity or outright dishonesty cannot be concealed. His conscience sees what he's up to, he senses his conscience seeing it, and guilt is the result.

✳   ✳   ✳

My description of the conscience highlights a feature that Freud underestimates in his theory of the superego. Although Freud carefully describes the voice of conscience, he gives short shrift to the eyes.[9] Yet *con-science,* properly so called, must share some intimate *knowledge with* the subject. What the conscience is thus privy to, I have suggested, is a backstage view of the subject's self-enactment and the social risks to which it exposes him.

Thus far, my description of the conscience also differs from Freud's with respect to the target of guilt. Freud says that guilt consists in anxiety about being punished by the conscience itself – that is, by the superego. Unfortunately, Freud is vague about the nature of the superego's punishments, and so the target of the subject's anxiety remains vague as well.[10] The form of guilt that I have described thus far consists in anxiety at the prospect of losing one's connection to other people, through the withdrawal of their willingness to engage in joint improvisation. The role of the conscience, I have said, is to remind the agent of that prospect.

Nevertheless, I think that the conscience does incite a further anxiety targeted directly at the conscience itself, and in this respect my description returns to Freud. In Freud's attempts to

[9] Freud does discuss this aspect of the conscience in at least one passage: "New Introductory Lectures," Lecture 31 (*The Standard Edition of the Complete Psychological Works of Sigmund Freud* [*S.E.*], ed. James Strachey et al. [London: The Hogarth Press], 22: 59–60, p. 66). Here he says that people with delusions of being watched are not mistaken, since there is a part of us all that watches us – the superego. (Thanks to Linda Brakel for the reference.)

[10] I discuss this problem in "A Rational Super-Ego?," *Philosophical Review* 108 (1999): 529–58; reprinted in *Self to Self,* 129–55.

specify the anxiety incited by the superego, he sometimes says that this anxiety echoes the subject's childhood fear of losing his parents' love.[11] This childhood fear reappears in the adult as anxiety about losing the love of his superego.

Remembering that the superego is a division of the self,[12] we can see that anxiety about losing the love of one's superego is in fact about losing one's own self-regard. It is akin to the desire to be able, as we say, to look at oneself in the mirror, or to look oneself in the eye – or, as Hume would say, to bear one's own survey.[13] The eyes by which one expects to be confronted in the mirror are like the eyes of one's conscience, whose favorable regard one wants to retain.

I think that Freud is correct to describe that favorable regard as love, though I also think that Freud's own conception of love is all wrong.[14] In order to complete my description of the conscience, I want to suggest a conception of love that might explain why the favorable regard of one's conscience might be so described. In particular, I want to explain why a person would even imagine the possibility of having, much less losing, the love of his conscience.

Clearly, the love at issue is not romantic love – the love of "being in love" or "falling in love." Nor is it the benevolent affection

---

[11] *Civilization and Its Discontents,* in *S.E.* 21: 59–145, p. 124; *New Introductory Lectures, S.E.* 22: 62; *An Outline of Psychoanalysis, S.E.* 23: 141–207, p. 206.

[12] Freud calls it "a differentiating grade in the ego" (e.g., in *Group Psychology and the Analysis of the Ego, S.E.*) 18: 65–143.

[13] *A Treatise of Human Nature,* Book III, section vi.

[14] I defend this claim in "Love as a Moral Emotion," *Ethics* 109 (1999): 338–74; reprinted in *Self to Self,* 70–109. See also my "Beyond Price," *Ethics* 118 (2008): 191–212. Here I discuss only one element of the view developed in those papers – the element corresponding to Murdoch's description of love as "an exercise of justice and realism and really *looking.*" Although I endorse that description, I think that it is very far from the whole story.

that comes out in the solicitous behavior of the "loving mothers" and "loving husbands" eulogized in standard obituaries. One may of course want "someone to watch over me," as the song says, but the watching over to be expected from the conscience is not of that sort: the conscience is not a caregiver.

There is, however, a variety of love that has struck some philosophers as involving attention such as might indeed be expected from the conscience. It is the love that Iris Murdoch describes as "an exercise of justice and realism and really *looking*,"[15] which leads to "the extremely difficult realization that something other than oneself is real."[16] This description of love is most plausible from the standpoint of the beloved. Being loved, we often feel, involves being attended to and *seen* – seen as we really are, unobscured by the wishes and fantasies of the viewer, on the one side, or by our own pretensions and dissimulations, on the other.

Among the things that others must see through, in order to see us as real, are the characters that we enact in the course of making ourselves intelligible. The reason why these characters need to be seen through is not that they are necessarily false or deceptive. In the ideal case, these characters are authentic, in that they represent who and what we really are as we enact them. The problem, to begin with, is that the actual case never fully attains the ideal: the characters we enact are the site of whatever self- and other-deception we may fall into. A deeper problem is that even if these characters are fully authentic, they are nevertheless incomplete, representing something that we really are but not everything that we have it in us to be. We always retain the sense that, behind our enacted selves, there stands a improviser

---

[15] *The Sovereignty of Good* (New York: Routledge and Kegan Paul, 1970), 91. I discuss Murdoch's view, and many other views of love, in "Love as a Moral Emotion."

[16] "The Sublime and the Good," in *Existentialists and Mystics: Writings on Philosophy and Literature*, ed. Peter Conradi (New York: Penguin, 1997), 205–20, p. 215.

struggling to articulate even more of himself – not a "more" that is already determinate, perhaps, but a "more" that could be made determinate in the enactment of a more richly articulated self. This self-enacter, and his as-yet-unenacted possibilities, are what we want someone to see when we want to be seen as we do in wanting to be loved.[17] To see *this*, however, would be to see the very process of self-enactment, as a process in which the self is being continually articulated and rearticulated. It is therefore to see the person, not from his own self-presenting and self-presented standpoint, but from a just and realistic standpoint of the sort that is occupied by his conscience.

That's why a loving gaze, though usually gratifying to the beloved, can also be threatening. The sense of being seen behind one's self-presentations isn't always a sense of validating recognition; it is sometimes a sense of naked exposure. Some people are afraid to be loved precisely because they are afraid to be so intimately seen: being loved is in some ways like having a conscience.[18]

During infancy, of course, the love between child and parents is a mixture of attachment, affection, and benevolence, emotions distinct from this particular form of unclouded attention. As a child approaches adolescence, however, his experience of love takes on aspects of the emotion that I am describing here – including, I believe, the desire to be truly seen, not as a character or characters enacted publicly, but as a self-enacter striving to articulate his still inchoate selves. At roughly the time when an adolescent begins to separate emotionally from his parents, he also begins to sense a self distinct from his outward identities,

---

[17] Relevant here are Charles Taylor's papers "What Is Human Agency?," in *The Self*, ed. Theodore Mischel (Totowa, NJ: Rowman and Littlefield, 1977), 103–35; and "Responsibility for Self," in *Free Will*, ed. Gary Watson (Oxford: Oxford University Press, 1982), 111–26.

[18] See Stanley Cavell's essay on King Lear, "The Avoidance of Love: A Reading of King Lear," in *Must We Mean What We Say? A Book of Essays* (Cambridge: Cambridge University Press, 1976), 267–353.

and to gain the sense that being loved entails being recognized and appreciated for himself. To be sure, an adolescent typically feels that no one sees his inner self, least of all his parents. But if all goes well, the internalized authorities, whoever they may be, are idealized as seeing into his heart, from their privileged interior vantage point.

The subject can then experience the gaze of his conscience as an "exercise of justice and realism and really *looking*" such as he craves in wanting to be loved. And what he fears from his conscience can be precisely the loss of this attention, a loss imagined as a turning away or an averting of the eyes. Even worse than the prospect that his conscience will scold or punish him is the prospect of its turning its back on him. And if his conscience really does turn its back on him, he may find himself all too able to look at himself in the mirror, since he will know that the most important pair of eyes is no longer looking.

My conception of the conscience explains why it is conceived as expressing moral concerns. Freud never fully explains why the superego criticizes and threatens to punish the subject for infractions of morality in particular. The superego described by Freud would be no more likely to berate the subject for stealing or lying than for having dirty fingernails, an infraction that may well have drawn parental discipline.

The reason why the conscience cares about right and wrong, I think, is that it occupies a perspective in which the fundamental doubleness of agency is especially salient. Viewing the subject from this perspective naturally raises questions such as who he purports to be, how he purports to live, whether his self-enactments are authentic, and whether they could serve as contributions to joint improvisation.

The conscience is not exclusively concerned with morality, however. It tends to address matters of faithfulness, in all senses of the term. In order to explain what I mean, I will need to make a digression into the topic of faithfulness to commitments.

∗ ∗ ∗

Often an agent has distant goals toward which his motivation can be expected to flag, or multiple goals that cannot be jointly attained. His present motivation for investing effort in attaining any of these goals, and hence the intelligibility of his doing so, depend on whether he can expect himself to persevere. If he expects his exertions to fluctuate with his momentary inclinations, he must sharply discount the expected return on present investments, and he may consequently find himself with no long-range projects in which it makes sense for him to invest. Choosing goals to which he can commit himself solves this problem, by giving him grounds for believing in future payoffs.

But how can a present commitment assure the agent that he will later follow through? The question almost answers itself. The agent knows that if he defaults on a commitment, he will undermine the credibility of his commitments, on which he relies for grounds to understand making investments in long-range goals. He can therefore rely on his future self to know that his reliability is on the line, and that he needs to demonstrate it so as to preserve his grounds for continuing to invest.

These grounds for self-reliance may seem self-deceptive. Usually when you try to give yourself evidence of having a particular motive, you end up giving yourself evidence of having a different one. You make a donation to charity in order to convince yourself of your own generosity, for example, thereby manifesting a self-serving motive instead. In order for this stratagem to satisfy you, some dishonesty must be involved.

In the present case, however, the agent isn't trying to give himself evidence of any particular motive – just some motive or other that can be trusted to make him follow through on commitments. And wanting evidence of a motive for following through on commitments is just such a motive, of which he can give himself evidence by doing so.

∗ ∗ ∗

It's just that simple, but it can also be spelled out in more complexity, as follows.

The agent desires evidence of his own reliability in fulfilling commitments, and he knows that he will go on desiring such evidence. If this desire could be relied on to motivate the fulfillment of commitments, it would constitute the very reliability of which it seeks evidence, and the behavior it motivates would constitute the evidence sought. The question is how the agent's desire for evidence of his own reliability can be relied on to motivate the fulfillment of commitments.

Well, suppose the agent believes that his fulfilling commitments counts as evidence of reliability even if it is motivated by his desire for such evidence. So long as he holds that belief, his desire for evidence of his own reliability will move him to fulfill commitments, in order to generate what he believes to be evidence of that reliability. And so long as his desire for evidence of his own reliability goes on moving him to fulfill commitments, it will constitute reliability on his part, and the behavior it motivates will count as evidence of that reliability. Provided that the desire continues moving him to fulfill commitments, then, his belief that fulfilling them is evidence of reliability will be true; and the desire will continue moving him to fulfill commitments provided that he continues to hold that belief.

The agent is therefore in a position to hold a self-fulfilling belief, to the effect that fulfilling commitments is evidence of reliability even if motivated by a desire for such evidence. Since he wants the belief to be true, and he can make it true by holding it, he does hold it, truly and with justification.[19]

✳ ✳ ✳

As the agent repeatedly makes and fulfills commitments to himself, his conscience sits as a silent witness to the process, preserving the memory of past commitments and watching for their fulfillment. As the agent lends and repays his self-trust, he may have motives for gullibility and deception; but his conscience is isolated from these motives, which belong to him in his capacities as audience and player. Here, too, the conscience serves as the impassive self-awareness that keeps him honest.

It keeps him honest not just with himself. For among his commitments to himself are those which he makes in the course of sincerely committing himself to others. No matter how sincerely the agent makes these interpersonal commitments, they are only as good as the intrapersonal commitments that underwrite their sincerity. That is, his promises to others are only as good as his intentions to fulfill them, which are commitments to himself. His deserving other people's trust therefore depends on deserving his own. In holding him to commitments, then, his conscience can sometimes hold him to moral obligations, though it can similarly hold him to a diet, a regimen of exercise, or even a criminal conspiracy.

Holding the agent to his commitments is one way in which his conscience prompts him to keep faith with himself. Another

---

[19] I thus suspect that skepticism about the rationality of proving one's reliability to oneself by fulfilling past commitments is based on skepticism about the rationality of adopting self-fulfilling beliefs. On the latter subject, see my "Epistemic Freedom," *Pacific Philosophical Quarterly* 70 (1989): 73–97; reprinted in *The Possibility of Practical Reason* (Oxford: Oxford University Press, 2000), 32–55.

way is by enforcing what are sometimes called volitional necessities.

∗ ∗ ∗

A person may feel categorically forbidden to do something because it is, as we say, unthinkable.[20] To say that it's unthinkable means, in my view, that he cannot find anything in his self-conception to make it intelligible as something that he would do. Contemplating this ostensible option, the improviser finds himself at a loss to make sense of his doing it; and so, as an agent, he is at a loss as to how he could do it, that is, how he could make it his doing.

Volitional necessities more often appear as things that we can't do than as things that we must. Something that we must do, volitionally speaking, is normally something toward which we are overwhelmingly inclined, and so it is the obvious thing to do, which we just do without a second thought. That we can't do something, however, we discover only after trying to see our way clear to doing it, by redescribing it and ourselves from various perspectives, hoping to see how it might appeal to us and how it might then make sense for us because of its appeal. Our not having it in us to do the thing is then a gradual discovery, which confronts us with the coercive force of necessity.

This improvisational version of writer's block is a backstage phenomenon, perceived by the self-enacter who finds a particular avenue closed to improvisation. It can only be guessed at by those who witness his outward performance, but it is visible to him, of course, and it is also visible to the eyes of his conscience. Necessities of this kind can therefore seem to be ratified by the conscience, which shares the subject's perception of

---

[20] Harry Frankfurt, "Rationality and the Unthinkable," in *The Importance of What We Care About* (Cambridge: Cambridge University Press, 1988), 177–90.

them, but they are not always moral requirements. A person can feel forbidden to eat meat – hence required to be a vegetarian – without thinking that others should be vegetarians; and he can feel unable to give up a vocation without thinking of it as a moral obligation at all (not, at least, in the moral philosopher's sense of 'moral'). Volitional necessities of this personal kind can be experienced as obligations and as enforced by the conscience, even though they are not about morality. They are obligations of faithfulness to oneself.

I thus think of the conscience as having a diverse portfolio – holding the self-presenter in its gaze, reminding him of his commitments, of his dependence on and vulnerability to fellow improvisers, and of the absolute limits on what he has it in him to do. These diverse functions generally provide moral motivation, but they also expose the agent to nonmoral shame and guilt, and to the force of his own character.

In reminding the subject of his vulnerability to social disqualification, the conscience will end up speaking on behalf of the socially accepted way of life. Here again I am agreeing with Freud, though not for Freudian reasons. Freud thinks that the superego demands obedience to social norms because it represents the subject's parents, who actually demanded obedience to those norms in particular. I am suggesting that the conscience speaks on behalf of social norms because it is experienced as seeing behind the subject's self-presentation and reminding him of his vulnerability to disqualification from social interaction. The upshot is the same, however: the conscience turns out to be conservative, in the first instance, defending the social status quo.

Since we cannot know a priori what way of life will be accepted by someone's society, we cannot say what specifically his conscience will tell him. We simply know that it will tell him more or less to toe the line. But is conscience limited to this conservative role? Can't it counsel rebellion against the local way of life?

Surely it can. When the local way of life requires something that the subject cannot find it in himself to do, his conscience may confirm his perception of being unable to do it. When this improvisational impossibility is due to values deeply entrenched in his character, it may be a moral impossibility, insofar as those values have been shaped by the pro-moral pressures of practical reason. A person may discover conflicts within the socially accepted way of life precisely because it asks him to do something that is incompatible with the values that he has acquired in support of it. And then his conscience will validate his sense of being categorically required to violate some social norms, in order to be true to the underlying values. His conscience may also validate his sense of being subject to requirements above and beyond social norms, insofar as he faces improvisational impossibilities that are purely personal.

Note, however, that departures from the going way of life must have the form of improvisational overtures, extended in the hope of gaining uptake from other improvisers.[21] A social innovation must be the proposal, however tacit, of *a role for me to play in our way of life*. It must therefore be suitable to serve as a shared premise for joint improvisation. And although an innovator may persist in taking a novel improvisational direction, he must be committed to the prospect of others' joining in, at least in the long run. (I will have more to say about this necessity in Lecture 6, when I discuss Kantian moral theory.)

Although volitional necessities are categorical, leaving the agent no intelligible alternative, they are not objectively certain. The fact that someone cannot find it in himself to do something does

---

[21] Here I borrow an idea from Kevin Toh.

not entail that it isn't there to be found, that no reframing of his self-understanding would make the act intelligible for him. There may well be a perspective from which the act would make sense even for the person he is now; it may simply be a perspective from which he hasn't yet considered the matter. And there will almost certainly be changes in himself that would make the act intelligible.

Thus, while I believe in these improvisational impossibilities, and the correlative practical necessities, I am also a fallibilist about our perception of them, and consequently a fallibilist about some deliverances of conscience. On the one hand, we must be prepared to find actions that are absolutely forbidden by who we are and how we live; on the other hand, we must also be prepared to reconsider what we seem to have found. Our judgments of practical necessity are not incorrigible.

Like the deliverances of scientific inquiry, those of practical inquiry can vary in their susceptibility to revision. There may be some courses of action that we could not find it in ourselves to pursue within any lives that would be remotely intelligible for creatures like ourselves. And we may be able to distinguish these strongly inaccessible courses of action from those whose rational inaccessibility is due to contingent features of our individual characters or local ways of life. The degree of certainty with which conscience speaks may therefore be variable, even when its dictates are categorical.

Finally, let me point out that my account of guilt has implications for the topic of punishment. If one purpose of punishment is to awaken a malefactor's conscience, then punishment should address what is of interest to the conscience, and what is of interest to the conscience, when it comes to possible punishments, is social disqualification. Another way of putting the same point is this: If guilt is, as Freud suggested, anxiety at the envisioned prospect of punishment, then social disqualification must be what constitutes punishment, according to my view.

The resulting conception of punishment is not that of inflicting pain or suffering on a malefactor in retribution for his misdeeds. Rather, it conceives of punishment as a matter of excluding a potential co-improviser from the collaborative process of joint improvisation, thereby excluding him from social interaction – in other words, shunning him, banning him, cutting him off, relegating him to social exile. The justification for punishment so conceived is not that it balances the scales of cosmic justice; the justification is that it is a perfectly sensible response of self-improvisers to someone who has proved incompetent or unreliable as a party to the collective improvisation. It is like sending a child to his room, or "giving him a time-out," because he has become unfit for participation in the shared activities of the family or the class.

This conception of punishment is intelligible only in light of the fact that all social interaction depends on the participants' reciprocal commitment to sharing a collective self-understanding as a basis on which to continue improvising together. The universal necessity of this commitment is what makes it possible to reject a bad actor as a potential inter-actor in any kind of interaction whatsoever. And that possibility is the object of the anxiety that constitutes the moral emotions of either shame or guilt, depending on the envisioned grounds of the rejection. Of course, shunning someone permanently and irrevocably will make no sense if he can allay doubts about his fitness for joint improvisation. That's why punishment should be tempered in the face of remorse, which displays the agent's susceptibility to the motives associated with conscience.

* * *

The conception of punishment outlined here does not require the concept of moral responsibility. People can be justified in refusing to share the social stage with a bad actor whether or not his unfitness as a co-improviser is his fault, whatever its being his fault might consist in. Assessments of fault are therefore unnecessary to the justification of that mode of punishment which is truly justified, according to my view.

Many philosophers believe that our ordinary concept of moral responsibility is essential to our sense of qualifying for the moral status of personhood.[22] Being a person, entitled to the respect of other persons, requires being potentially responsible for our actions, according to this view. Our capacity to be at fault in our treatment of others is what makes it possible for others to be at fault in their treatment of us, and this mutual susceptibility to fault is the basis of our moral standing. Without it, we would no longer be entitled to respect, either from others or, by the same token, from ourselves. So many philosophers believe.

I grant that conditions of responsibility must be attached to legal punishment, because it carries the coercive power of the state. The loss of freedom entailed in exposure to state coercion must be mitigated by the requirement that such coercion be applied only as a foreseeable response to actions chosen freely. Our entitlement to political freedom thus yields a right to be subject to no social control more intrusive than punishment on the basis of responsibility. In that sense, the concept of responsibility is essential to our legal or political status as persons.

But I reject the view that our moral status as persons depends on the concept of moral responsibility. I believe that I have outlined a conception of persons as proper objects of moral consideration without invoking our capacity for moral responsibility. (I will have more to say in defense of this claim in subsequent lectures.)The mutual regard that is required of collaborating self-improvisers, and hence of any parties to human interaction,

---

[22] The *locus classicus* for a view like this is Peter Strawson, "Freedom and Resentment," in *Freedom and Resentment and Other Essays* (London: Methuen, 1974), 1–25.

is sufficient to animate moral relations among us. In my view, we would do better to leave the concept of responsibility out of our merely social dealings.

✳ ✳ ✳

This concludes my description of rational agents and their inter-actions. In the following lectures I will turn from description to theory. In Lecture 5, I will consider how my conception of ratio-nal agency allows for the objectivity of morality, by allowing for the objectivity of practical reasoning. At the end of that lecture, I will argue that practical reasoning is an empirical discipline, whose findings cannot be foreseen from the confines of the philosophical study. This argument will raise the question why so many philosophers have sought to anticipate the findings of practical reasoning, by propounding normative theories. The status of normative theory will be my topic in Lecture 6. Lecture 7 will be devoted to a discontinuity in practical reasoning, aris-ing from a discontinuity between modes of self-understanding. I will argue that the discontinuity corresponds to the distinction between the goodness and the meaningfulness of a person's life.

5

Foundations

Consider another picture of what it would be for a demand to be 'objectively valid'. It is Kant's own picture. According to this, a demand will be inescapable in the required sense if it is one that a rational agent must accept if he is to be a rational agent. It is, to use one of Kant's favourite metaphors, *self-addressed* by any rational agent. Kant was wrong, in my view, in supposing that the fundamental demands of morality were objective in this sense, but that is not the immediate point, which is that the conception deploys an intelligible and adequate sense of objectivity. It seems to have little to do with those demands being part of the fabric of the world; or, at any rate, they will be no more or less so than the demands of logic – which was, of course, part of Kant's point.

Bernard Williams, "Ethics and the Fabric of the World"[1]

In explaining how the demands of morality can be objective without being "part of the fabric of the world," Bernard Williams

This lecture deals with problems that have been treated inadequately in my earlier work, as has been pointed out to me, repeatedly and with stoic patience, by Nishi Shah, Nadeem Hussain, Kieran Setiya, and Matty Silverstein. Others who have helped with this material include David Enoch, Melis Erdur, David Plunkett, and Sharon Street.

[1] In *Making Sense of Humanity and Other Philosophical Papers 1982–1993* (Cambridge: Cambridge University Press, 1995), 172–81.

is responding to John Mackie, who thinks that being woven into that fabric is a necessary condition for objectivity.[2] Williams points out that moral demands might be woven into the practical point of view instead. Anyone to whom they are addressed must already occupy that point of view and must therefore accept whatever demands are woven into it. Morality might thus be objective without meeting Mackie's condition.

"The fabric of the world" is of course a metaphor. The fabric of the world is what satisfies indicative judgments, thereby making them true, or fails to satisfy them, thereby making them false. But a demand is an imperative – "Do it!" – which cannot be true or false. In order for a demand to be woven into the world, there would have to be a corresponding judgment that could be made true by the worldly fabric – say, the judgment "It ought to be done." Whatever made this judgment true would make the corresponding demand objectively valid, in Mackie's view.

The alternative view outlined by Williams forgoes the step of transposing demands into indicative judgments. It leaves them in their practical form, as demands – or at least as practical thoughts of some kind, such as aims or commitments or policies. The view contends that such practical thoughts can be objectively valid without having indicative proxies that are made true by swatches of the world: practical thoughts can be objectively valid by being inescapable, in the sense that any agent must accept them.

The point is to show that we can account for the objectivity of morality without positing a normative reality of which judgments of right and wrong can be true. The point is not to disprove the existence of such a reality but merely to show that we don't need it in order to explain how morality can be objective.

Williams attributes this strategy to Kant, and I will follow him by calling it the Kantian strategy. But Williams does not himself adopt the strategy, because he does not believe that the practical point of view incorporates the demands of morality or any other demands from which they could be derived. Having criticized

[2] *Ethics: Inventing Right and Wrong* (Harmondsworth: Penguin Books, 1977).

Mackie for overlooking a way in which morality might be objective, Williams concludes that it isn't objective in that way, after all.

* * *

I share Williams's pessimism, but I don't think that the Kantian strategy should be completely abandoned. In this lecture, I will try to explain how the demands of morality might be supported by something that is woven into the practical point of view, even if moral demands themselves are not.

My version of the Kantian strategy will rely on the theory of practical reasoning that I have developed in the preceding lectures. Applying that theory to questions about the foundations of morality will raise some foundational questions about the theory itself – for example, whether it characterizes practical reasoning as subjective or objective. I will address these questions before returning to the objectivity of morality.

To begin with, however, I am going to set my theory of practical reasoning to one side, in order to frame the foundational questions in their most general form, without any preconceptions about the nature of action or practical reason. I will retain the assumption, shared by virtually all writers on the subject, that our doings amount to actions rather than mere behavior when and only when they are done for reasons. I will draw various implications from this constitutive relation between reasons and actions, mainly following Bernard Williams. But the rest of my theory will sit temporarily in abeyance while I frame the foundational questions.

After framing those questions, I will briefly reintroduce my theory, taking this opportunity to highlight some features that may have been lost in the details of the previous lectures. I will then consider the foundations of my theory and, finally, foundational questions about morality.

* * *

First, then, the objectivity of practical reasoning – another question on which Bernard Williams is something of a skeptic. His skepticism is a version of Humean skepticism, according to which practical reason is no more than a "slave of the passions."

Williams claims that reasons for acting[3] must be "internal" in the sense that they must be geared to some element of the agent's "subjective motivational set" – that is, some subjective inclination that the agent already has.[4] His argument for this claim is that a reason for someone to act must be such that the person could rationally come to act on the basis of it; and in order to act on the basis of a reason, the person would have to act under the influence of that reason, an influence that it can exert only by engaging one of his motives at the time of action. If the person currently has no motive that could be engaged by a consideration, he may yet acquire one through delibera-tion; but if sound deliberation wouldn't bring him to have such

---

[3] In this lecture, I speak of "reasons for acting" and "acting for reasons," although I find these locutions potentially misleading. I would prefer to speak of acting "for reason" (in the singular), a locution modelled on "for cause" in the report of an employee's termination. When we terminate an employee for cause, we may be required to itemize the relevant cause or causes, but they are usually abstracted from a holistic *Gestalt* of incompe-tence or dereliction that is not just their sum. (A requirement to itemize them may of course serve important purposes nonetheless.) Similarly, when we act for reason, as I would prefer to say, we are influenced by a holis-tic conception self, situation, and action from which itemizable reasons can at best be abstracted, usually after the fact.

[4] The remainder of this section reprises the argument of my paper "The Possibility of Practical Reason," *Ethics* 106 (1996): 694–726; reprinted in *The Possibility of Practical Reason* (Oxford: Oxford University Press, 2000), 170–99. For Williams's view, see his "Internal and External Reasons," in *Moral Luck* (Cambridge: Cambridge University Press, 1981), 101–13; "Internal Reasons and the Obscurity of Blame," in *Making Sense of Humanity*, 35–45; and "Replies," in *World, Mind, and Ethics: Essays on the Ethical Philosophy of Bernard Williams*, ed. J. E. J. Altham and Ross Harrison (Cambridge: Cambridge University Press, 1995), 185–224.

a motive, then he could not rationally come to be influenced by the consideration, and so he could not rationally come to act on it. The consideration would consequently be disqualified from being a reason for him to act.

Williams assumes that which motives an agent could come to have through sound deliberation depends on which motives he already has, because deliberation merely conveys an agent from one motive to another: it requires a motive as input in order to yield a motive as output. Williams therefore concludes that an agent's existing motives determine which considerations he could rationally come to act on, which are the only considerations that can qualify as reasons for him to act. The reasons there can be for a person to act are thus constrained by the motives that he already happens to have, and those motives are "subjective" – presumably, in the sense that other agents may have different motives without anyone's being mistaken, rationally speaking. Similarly situated agents may therefore have different reasons for acting, because of having different motivational susceptibilities.[5]

I agree with Williams's premise that reasons for acting must be able to engage a motive that the agent has or could come to have through sound deliberation; and I do not wish to question the assumption that deliberation can convey him only from

---

[5] Here I should distinguish between two senses in which reasons might be objective. Some philosophers have thought that reasons for acting are objective in the sense that they militate for or against outcomes, whose promotion or prevention they recommend indiscriminately to everyone, irrespective of his circumstances. (See Thomas Nagel, *The Possibility of Altruism* [Princeton, NJ: Princeton University Press, 1970], Chapter 10.). Williams would deny that reasons for acting are objective in this sense, but his main point is to deny that they are objective in a further sense, in which they seem more likely to be objective. For even if an agent's circumstances can give him reasons privately, so to speak, without generating reasons for other agents, they may do so objectively in the sense that others *would* have similar reasons *if* they were in similar circumstances. According to Williams, however, whether agents in similar circumstances would have similar reasons depends on whether they have similar motives that their circumstances could engage.

motive to motive, so that his current motives determine where he could rationally end up. But I reject Williams's conclusion, that reasons must therefore be geared to something subjective in the agent's motivational makeup.

For suppose that there is a single motive that any reason must engage in order for an agent to act on the basis of it. A creature will need this motive in order to satisfy the prerequisite for being subject to reasons for acting – in order for there to be reasons *for* him, or *applicable to* him – but he will then satisfy that prerequisite with respect to any and all possible reasons. Variance in motivation will no longer entail that similarly situated agents can have different reasons, depending on how they can come to be motivated by their similar situations; it will entail only that some creatures but not others can have reasons at all, because only some can be motivated in the relevant way.[6] Any creature lacking the relevant motive will be immune to the influence of reasons for acting and hence exempt from their application. There certainly are such creatures – lower animals, for example. Lower animals aren't subject to reasons because they are constitutionally incapable of being influenced by them. A rational agent will differ from such a creature, under this supposition, by having a motive that makes him susceptible to and therefore subject to reasons; and this motive will make him susceptible to reasons in general, not just to those which engage motives peculiar to him.

This motive will have to incline the agent, upon considering reasons, to do that for which they are reasons, and indeed to do it

---

[6] A complication here is that the relevant circumstances may include the agent's psychological state, which includes his motives. So considered, a motive can be an objective reason, if it counts as a reason for anyone similarly motivated. If its role is rather to make its possessor susceptible to the influence of some further circumstances, so that they can be reasons for him but not for others similarly circumstanced, then it helps to constitute subjective reasons. Williams's claim is that motives play the latter role in the constitution of reasons.

because of their being reasons for it.[7] But which considerations qualify as reasons for acting, and how do they qualify?

Some philosophers think that we cannot characterize reasons for acting more informatively than as "considerations that favor an action."[8] I doubt whether the notion of favoring an

[7] Note that the 'because' in this sentence is not the 'because' of rationalizing explanation. That is, the creature does not, in the normal case, perform the action recommended by reasons *on the grounds of* their being reasons for it; the creature performs the action *in response to* their being reasons for it – or, to be more precise, in response to that in virtue of which they are reasons. (For an explanation of this last qualification, see note 23, below.)

[8] See, e.g., Thomas M. Scanlon, *What We Owe to Each Other* (Cambridge, MA: Belknap Press, 1999), Chapter 1; and Jonathan Dancy, *Ethics Without Principles* (Oxford: Clarendon Press, 2004). Actually, what Scanlon says is that a reason for something is "a consideration that *counts* in favor of it" (p. 4, my italics). Scanlon thinks that the idea of counting in favor of something needs no explanation; I disagree.

Counting is not, in the first instance, something that considerations do; it's something that people do. (See Matthew Silverstein, "Ethics as Practical," [MS], p. 8.) Counting is an activity, and it is an essentially rule-governed activity. It is governed by rules for adding to a sum, or subtracting from it, in accordance with items of some kind, individuated in some way. When we speak of things rather than people as counting, we mean that those things are *to be counted* under such a set of rules. When the students ask, "Does spelling count?," they are asking whether the rules for grading their work provide for points to be added or subtracted for words spelled correctly or incorrectly. When we say, "Close doesn't count in horseshoes," we're talking about the rules for scoring the game.

The rules under which spelling counts on an assignment need not be fully determinate, but they cannot be utterly formless, either. If bad spelling merely has some probability of lowering a student's grade by putting the teacher into a bad mood, we would not say that spelling counts; we would say that it makes a difference but not by "counting." In order for spelling to count, there has to be some method for counting it, however vague or imprecise that method may be.

To speak of considerations as counting in favor of an action therefore raises the question, How do they count? The expression presupposes that there is a method governed by rules, however vague and imprecise, for scoring or grading actions by enumerating pros and cons. Rather than obviate further explanation, this expression underscores the need for one. Talk

action can stand without further explanation. It might stand without further explanation, I suppose, if "considerations" were taken to include evaluative judgments, such as the judgment that an action would be an apt or fitting or correct thing to do, a judgment that clearly does favor the action, by evaluating it favorably. The problem is that such evaluative considerations cannot be self-standing, since aptness or correctness cannot be primitive properties of an action. That is, an action cannot be simply apt or correct; it must be apt or correct in virtue of having some other properties; and those properties of the action are then what qualify as reasons for taking it. Reasons, in other words, do not favor an action by *evaluating* it favorably; they favor it by describing it in other ways that support a favorable evaluation.

The favorable evaluation that reasons support, I have suggested, is that the action is "apt" or "fitting" or "correct."[9] Another equivalent for these terms is the archaic sense of 'just' that supplies the root of the verb 'to justify'. To indicate that an action is apt or fitting or correct is to justify it, and the considerations that qualify as reasons for an action must be considerations that justify it in this sense.

How is the justificatory force of reasons related to their motivational force? Reasons are considerations that support the

of considerations as "counting in favor" is empty unless there is something further to be said about how they count. Hence such talk can be the beginning but not the end of theorizing about reasons. (These remarks about "counting" can also be applied *mutatis mutandis* to "weighing" and any other operational metaphors that are used to forestall inquiry into reasons.)

9 I will try to keep both "apt" and "correct" in play, because the latter strikes my ear as drawing an all-or-nothing distinction, whereas the mode of aptness or correctness at issue in practical reasoning is in my view a matter of degree.

evaluation of an action as apt or correct, and can move the agent toward the action, ultimately becoming the reasons for which he performs it. But are they capable of moving the agent toward the action because they support a favorable evaluation of it, or do they support that evaluation because they are somehow capable of moving him?

We might try to answer this question with two others: How else could an agent be moved by reasons, if not because he recognizes that they justify action? And how could he be moved by that recognition unless it was already true? In the face of these questions, we might conclude that justification must come first in the order of constitution.

This much at least is true: the motivational force of reasons must be systematically related to their justificatory force. It's not enough for considerations to influence an agent in any old way – for example, by making him jump when they're shouted next to his ear. In that case, he would not have acted on the basis of those considerations, even if they were reasons for jumping. He acts on the basis of considerations, for the reasons they afford, only when his being influenced by them is connected nonaccidentally with their justifying what he does.

But must this nonaccidental connection be one of priority, of the agent's being influenced by reasons because he recognizes that they justify? That is the question.

The answer is no. We should resist the temptation to assume that reasons for acting owe their influence to the agent's recognizing them as justifying action.

If reasons owed their influence to being recognized as justifiers, then the motive needed to bring behavior under their influence would be a motive toward doing what's justified, so described. Yet there still has to be a substantive criterion of aptness or correctness in relation to which actions can be justified. They can't be justified merely in relation to the formal criterion of being justified: such a criterion would be vacuous. Justification requires a substantive criterion, specifying what kinds of action are apt or correct, or "just" in the archaic sense. Reasons must justify in relation to some such criterion, by indicating that an action has the features therein specified as criterial of aptness or correctness. And such reasons will be able to engage a motive explicitly directed at those features – a motive toward the kinds of action specified as apt or correct or just, rather than a motive toward doing what's justified, so described. By engaging that substantive motive, reasons can motivate action nonaccidentally, in a manner systematically connected to their justificatory force. They can thereby exert the right kind of influence to serve as the basis for action, and so they need not owe that influence to being recognized as justifiers.

Thus, reasons must be considerations that indicate an action to meet a substantive criterion that is a criterion of aptness or correctness. And they can exert their influence, in the first instance, by engaging a substantive motive toward meeting that criterion, without being seen as justifying that for which they are reasons.

Consider by way of analogy the process by which reasons for believing something lead a subject to believe it.[10] Reasons for believing that p are considerations indicating that this belief would meet the relevant criterion of correctness, which is truth. But a subject rarely considers the question whether a belief in p would be correct or even whether it would be true; rather, he considers the question whether p, and his attitude toward p is then responsive to considerations indicating either that p or that not-p. The influence of reasons on his beliefs depends on his disposition to believe a proposition in response to considerations indicating it to be true and hence correct to believe, but

[10] For a relevant discussion of this analogy, see Peter Railton, "On the Hypothetical and Non-Hypothetical in Reasoning about Belief and Action," in *Ethics and Practical Reason*, ed. Garrett Cullity and Berys Gaut (Oxford: Clarendon Press, 1997), 53–79.

he needn't make the "semantic ascent" of explicitly considering the issues of truth or correctness.[11]

Well and good. But what is the substantive criterion of correctness for actions? What is it to act correctly?

We can supply a criterion of correctness for any particular action by directing it at a contingent aim – an aim that is contingent in the sense that the action might or might not be directed at it while still retaining its nature as an action. I can flip a switch with the aim of thereby illuminating a room, and then my action can be correct or incorrect as a means to achieving that aim; but I could have flipped the switch without having that aim, which is therefore contingent in relation to my action. Promoting the room's illumination is thus a criterion of aptness for my action only contingently.

There is a view according to which this mode of correctness, relative to a contingent aim, is the only mode of correctness to be found in the practical sphere. In this respect, actions and aims are taken to differ from beliefs, which, by being true or false, can be correct or incorrect merely as beliefs, irrespective of any further role that they may happen to play. If I believe that a switch controls the light, then my belief is correct if true, and incorrect if false, whether or not it is relevant to the achievement of my aims; whereas the correctness or incorrectness of flipping the switch depends on what I aim to achieve by doing so.

---

[11] Even the question whether *p* need not come up for consideration. The subject may simply come to believe that *p* in response to considerations indicating that *p*, without ever having raised the question – indeed, without having focused attention on *p* or the considerations that bear on it. Still, his belief is formed in response to indications of its truth, via a disposition to meet a criterion specifying what is correct for beliefs.

The problem is that if an action can be apt or inapt only in relation to a contingent aim, then its justification may seem to be incomplete until the aim itself is justified. And according to the present view, an aim is like an action in that it can be apt only in relation to a contingent aim – presumably a further aim – on which it therefore depends for its justification. I can justify flipping the switch as a means of illuminating the room, and I can justify illuminating the room as a means of finding my keys; and I can justify finding my keys as a means of starting the car; but no matter how long I go on with such justifications, I will always feel obliged to go further, so as to justify the latest aim in the series, which will be a further but still contingent aim at which I happen to have directed my action. The present view therefore seems to yield a dilemma: the justification of action must either lead to an infinite regress of justifications or stop short at a contingent aim that remains unjustified.[12]

---

[12] We might avoid the present dilemma by revising our assumption that all practical justification must be in relation to a contingent aim. We might think instead that an ultimate aim – an aim not subordinate to any ulterior aim – can be justified on the grounds of belonging to a complete set of ultimate aims that are mutually coherent. (For this view, see Sharon Street, "Constructivism about Reasons," in *Oxford Studies in Metaethics*, Vol. 3, ed. Russ Shafer-Landau (New York: Oxford University Press, 2008), 207–45.

To this suggestion, I reply that we will then have posited a criterion of correctness for ultimate aims, namely, coherence. And with that clarification, I accept the suggestion, since my version of the Kantian strategy has the suggested form. The criterion of correctness that I will propose is a species of coherence, not just for aims but for all other evaluative attitudes and for actions as well. I will argue that this particular criterion is entrenched in the very nature of agency.

You might wonder, Isn't a demand for coherent aims objectively valid anyway, whether or not it is entrenched in the nature of agency? I think not. It would be objectively valid if our aims could be couched in value judgments that aimed to be true, since incoherent judgments cannot be true simultaneously. But if we are seeking to explain the objectivity of practical thought without positing states of affairs that make it true, we cannot

Some philosophers think that a result of this sort is unavoidable in the practical sphere; but we would of course prefer to avoid it, so as to avoid concluding that practical justification must either go on forever or stop short. The way to avoid it would be to show that actions can be justified as such, in the manner of beliefs – justified independently of any contingent aim at which they might be directed.[13] In order for actions to be justifiable as such, however, they would need a criterion of aptness or correctness that isn't contingent, a criterion that applies to them simply in virtue of their being actions, just as the criterion of truth applies to beliefs simply in virtue of their being beliefs. So we have reason to look for a criterion of aptness or correctness embedded in the very nature of action.

In sum, if we want to avoid concluding that practical justification is either endless or abortive, we should look for a substantive criterion of aptness or correctness in relation to which actions can be justified as such.[14] Reasons for performing an action will then be considerations that justify it in relation to that criterion, and if a creature is motivated to meet the criterion, they will be able to influence him in such a way as to become the reasons for which he acts. What makes the creature motivationally susceptible to any particular reason will be, not a contingent element of his motivational set, but a motive that makes him susceptible to reasons in general. Now, a motive that makes a creature susceptible to the influence of reasons in general will there by

ground a demand for coherence on the relation between coherence and truth. (On this topic, see the end of Lecture 2.)

[13] The emphasis in this clause is on the word 'contingent'. My version of the Kantian strategy concedes that actions must be justified in relation to an aim; it simply asserts that this aim is inherent in the nature of action and is consequently not contingent in relation to agency.

[14] Compare Ralph Wedgwood, *The Nature of Normativity* (Oxford: Clarendon Press, 2007), 51 ff. Wedgwood's notion of a "winning" action is similar to my notion of an apt or correct action. See also my paper "The Possibility of Practical Reason."

make him capable of acting rather than merely behaving, since action is behavior performed for reasons. If reasons for him to act can engage such a motive, they will not have to rely on contingent elements of his motivational set; they can rely instead on a motive constitutive of his very agency.

*   *   *

I have just said this: that if we can find a substantive criterion of correctness for action, then we will have found a motive that can mediate the influence of all reasons for acting, a motive that will constitute agency itself rather than a subjective element in the motivational makeup of only some agents. What I really want to say, however, is the converse: that if we can find a motive that's constitutive of agency, then we will have found a substantive criterion of correctness for action. For I think that the criterion of correctness for action must depend on what action is, and hence on the nature of agency, rather than vice versa.

You may now suspect me of putting the cart before the horse. Which motive makes one an agent, you may think, must depend on which motive makes one susceptible to reasons; which must depend (you think) on which considerations qualify as reasons, by justifying action; which must depend (you think) on the criterion of correctness for action as such. But think again. Admittedly, we got the idea of a motive that constitutes agency by wondering which considerations qualify as reasons. But we don't have to derive the nature of that motive from the nature of reasons; we can now work in the other direction.[15] What justifies actions depends on what they are constitutively motivated

---

[15] I cleared the way for working in this direction when I argued, a moment ago, that the motivational influence of reasons does not depend on their being recognized as justifying action. If it did, then their status as justifiers could not depend, as I shall now argue, on the motive that mediates their influence.

toward, which can be discovered independently of the nature of reasons, as I have already explained in my first lecture. Here I am simply reversing the expected order of explanation in the same way I did in Lectures 1 and 2.

What I said in Lecture 1 is that the autonomous agent is like an actor improvising an enactment of the character who he actually is – or, rather, the character who he becomes in improvising an enactment of him. Improvisation can serve as a model for action, I claimed, because the behavior that rises to the status of action is the behavior that we make up as we go along. And the considerations whose guidance constitutes our behaviour as improvisation – as made up and hence as action – thereby qualify as reasons for acting, because action just is behavior performed for reasons.

* * *

Let me reintroduce this theory by borrowing from the book that inaugurated contemporary philosophy of action, G. E. M. Anscombe's *Intention*.[16] I will return to foundational questions after reintroducing my theory.

Anscombe formulated the contrast between action and mere behavior in terms of two thoughts about the future. Her examples were the thoughts "I am going to be sick" and "I am going to take a walk."[17] The latter thought embodies a decision to take a walk, but the former doesn't embody a decision to be sick; it's a prediction, not a decision.[18] Anscombe explained the difference

---

[16] As I explained in note 1 of Lecture 1, I am speaking only of distinctively human action, allowing for the possibility that the concept of action is realized differently in organisms of other kinds.

[17] Actually, Anscombe drew the contrast between statements, but focusing on the thoughts is simpler.

[18] Actually, Anscombe used 'prediction' as the generic term for both statements; her term for the former was 'estimate of the future', which she contrasted with 'intention'.

in terms of the causal order between the thoughts and the states
of affairs that they represent. The disposition to be sick causes
the thought "I am going to be sick," whereas the thought "I am
going to take a walk" causes the disposition to take a walk.

Here Anscombe pinpointed the sense in which we make
up our autonomous actions but not our other behavior. The
contrast lies in how we stand in relation to our behavior in
forethought about it. When the fact that we are going to do
something makes us think so, then we clearly have not made it
up; the case in which we have made up the fact that we are going
to do something is the case in which our thinking it makes it
so. And in the latter case but not the former, our behavior will
amount to an autonomous action.

This contrast is analogous to that between reading and writing: "I am going to be sick" is a *reading* of the speaker's future,
whereas "I am going to take a walk" is a case of *writing* it. That's
why we think of ourselves as the authors of our actions but not of
our other behavior. And it's also the respect in which we resemble improvisational actors, who are the authors of what they do
onstage.

The order of causation between autonomous action and forethought about it accounts for the openness of the future in the
eyes of autonomous agents.[19] If by thinking "I am going to take
a walk" you can make it so – and if you can also make it *not* so by
thinking its negation – then your thoughts are not answerable
to any fact of the matter, even if there is one.

---

[19] I discuss this phenomenon in "Epistemic Freedom," *Pacific Philosophical
Quarterly* 70 (1989): 73–97; reprinted in *The Possibility of Practical Reason*,
32–55. See also James M. Joyce, "Are Newcombe Problems Really
Decisions?," *Synthese* 156 (2007): 537–62.

Let the fact of the matter be that you are going to take a walk: that fact must be partly due to the prior fact that you are not going to think otherwise; for if you were going to think otherwise, then you would subsequently do otherwise. Hence the fact that you are going to take a walk cannot rationally oblige you to think so, since you would be perfectly correct in thinking not, which would cause you not to take the walk instead. So even if there is a fact of the matter as to whether you will take a walk, you may think whatever you like on the matter without fear of getting it wrong. There is something that you are actually going to think – namely, that you are going to take a walk – which is what will cause you to take a walk, as *ex hypothesi* you are going to. But what will prompt the thought that you are going to take a walk cannot be the fact that you are going to, since you know that this fact depends on the thought rather than vice versa. What will prompt you to think that you are going to take a walk, given your entitlement to think whatever you like, is that you'd like to take a walk.

The result is that you are obliged – condemned, if it comes to that – to make up your future course of action. Try as you might to read your future, you will unavoidably be writing it, since it will be caused by the thoughts in which you purport to read it, and it would turn out differently if those thoughts were different. Without self-deception, then, you cannot purport to read your future at all. Like an improvisational actor who can find no script to read from, you can find no facts to read from, when it comes to your future actions.

I think that Anscombe was correct to see autonomy in the relation between our actions and our forethought about them. My conception of agency, which was outlined in Lecture 1, elaborates on Anscombe's insight by spelling out the relevant thought and its relation to action.

Consider the thought by which we attempt to read someone else's forthcoming action. It's a thought about the circumstances, attitudes, and attributes of his that would account for his doing one thing rather than another. That's how the audience of a drama tries to anticipate the next move of a character: they try to figure out what it would make sense for him to do next. If the drama is scripted, of course, then the actor knows more than the audience about his character's next move, but he still shares their passive relation to it. He has read the character's next move in the script, whereas they must try to read it by extrapolation from the dramatic action thus far; but he and they are alike in occupying the position of readers.

If the drama is improvised, however, then the actor thinks along the same lines as the audience, about what it would make sense for his character to do next, since that's how he must think in order to act "in character." The former difference between audience and actor disappears, then, but a new one appears in its place. Now the difference is that the thoughts of the audience are reading the character's future, whereas the actor's thoughts are writing it, since what he does next as the character will be determined by what he thinks it would make sense for the character to do. In wondering what his character *would* do under the dramatic circumstances – what it would be in character for him to do – the actor cannot take himself to be speculating about what his character is going to do anyway; he must realize that his character is going to do whatever he, the actor, thinks it would be in character for him to do, that being what the actor is looking to enact in order to maintain the character. In thinking about what the character would do, the actor is writing the character's actions rather than reading them.

So it is with an autonomous agent, as I conceive him. When the agent thinks about what it would make sense for him to do in light of his circumstances, attitudes, and attributes, he cannot honestly purport to be reading his future in them, since what he does is going to depend on what he sees as making sense in light of them. His preexisting motives will be joined, and their balance potentially altered, by the very motive that leads him to think about them as clues to his next action, since that motive will incline him to do what those clues render it most intelligible for him to do. The very thoughts by which the agent might try to read his future are thus thoughts by which he cannot help but write it, because they will help to determine how the balance of his motives will tip.[20] And the agent thereby comes to resemble an actor who writes his own words and actions in the course of performing them.

Returning now to the analogy with belief, we might say that whereas belief consists in the truth-seeking acceptance of a proposition – an acceptance that follows indications of what's actually true – action consists in behavior that follows considerations that make it intelligible to the agent. Action is thus behavior aimed at intelligibility, just as belief is acceptance aimed at truth.

Now, a subject who lacked a disposition to follow indications of truth would not be capable of forming beliefs. He could accept that p – that is, regard p as true – but his acceptance would float free of indications as to whether p was true in actuality. And, because his acceptance of p would not look to actuality, it would count as fantasy or hypothesizing or idle speculation rather than

---

[20] As I explained in Lecture 1, candor requires that, in taking some move to be intelligible, the agent take it to be intelligible in light of his circumstances, attitudes, attributes, *and his hereby taking it to be intelligible* – to be intelligible, then, as a move that he is writing rather than reading with this very thought. For if he took something else to make more sense, the balance of his motives would be tipped in its direction – in light of which it really would make more sense, and as a result of which he would do it instead.

belief.[21] The capacity to believe thus requires a susceptibility to
indications of truth.

We might even suspect that this prerequisite for the attitude of
belief is what makes truth its criterion of correctness.[22] What constitutes a belief, we might think, is the truth-seeking acceptance of
a proposition – an acceptance that follows indications of truth. The
reason why a belief is correct if and only if true, we might add, is that
it's correct if and only if it succeeds at reaching what it constitutively
seeks, by way of its responsiveness to truth-relevant considerations.

The analogous conclusion about action would be that its criterion of correctness is intelligibility, because intelligibility is its
constitutive aim.[23] I accept this conclusion. Now I claim that the
criterion of correctness for action is how it would make sense to

---

[21] I argue for this claim at length in "On the Aim of Belief", in *The Possibility
of Practical Reason*, 244–81.

[22] This isn't the complete story about belief, in my view. For more, see Nishi
Shah and J. David Velleman, "Doxastic Deliberation," *Philosophical Review*
114 (2005): 497–534. There we elaborate on Shah's view (put forward in
his "How Truth Governs Belief," *Philosophical Review* 112 [2003]: 447–82)
that the truth-seeking tendency of belief is not sufficient to ground its criterion of correctness, and that the criterion must therefore be implicit in
the concept of belief. In note 24, below, I explain why I think that the constitutive aim of action, unlike that of belief, can ground the corresponding
criterion of correctness.

[23] Here there are two subtly different explanations, running in opposite
directions. On the one hand, an agent acts because of being influenced by
reasons; on the other hand, considerations qualify as reasons because they
are of the sort whose influence turns behavior into action. The latter explanation blocks a tempting elaboration on the former. What explains the
action can be the fact that the agent is influenced by their being reasons
but not that he is influenced by the fact that they *are* reasons. For if they had
to qualify as reasons before they could exert the influence that turns behavior into action, then their power to exert that influence could not be what
made them reasons. They would have to qualify as reasons first in order to
exert their action-constituting influence, and so their qualifying as reasons
couldn't depend on their power to exert it.

(continued on page 135)

behave, because action consists in behavior that aims at making sense, by being sensitive to considerations of its own intelleg-ibility, which therefore qualify as reasons for acting. In Lecture 2, I claimed that the criterion of correctness for valuing is what it would make sense to respond to in some way, because valuing always consists in a response that aims at making sense, by being sensitive to considerations of its own intelligibility, which there-fore quality as reasons for valuing in that way. I will now argue for this claim by defending it against various objections.

You may object that showing a particular aim to be constitu-tive of action is not sufficient to show that it sets a criterion of aptness or correctness for action. Achieving the aim may be

I thus arrive at a complex response to the Euthyphro problem (with the help of Matthew Evans; see his "The Lessons of Euthyphro 10a-11b," MS). Plato's argument in the *Eythyphro* shows that nothing can be pious simply because the gods love it. By the same token, however, the gods don't love anything simply because it is pious; they love it because it has features that make it pious. And now a second order-of-explanation question arises. Do features make something pious because they are the ones for which the gods love it? Or do the gods love it for those features because they are pious-making? The correct order of explanation is the former. The gods love what is pious because of the features that make it pious, but those features make it pious because they are the ones for which the gods love it. Hence the gods love what is pious because of the features that make it pious but not because of their making it so.

These explanations can run in different directions because they explain in different ways. When we say that the gods love something because of what makes it pious, we are giving a causal explanation: pious-making fea-tures elicit the gods' love. When we say that the features are pious-making because they elicit the gods' love, we are giving a constitutive or conceptual explanation: to be elicitive of divine love is what it is to be pious-making. (I believe that this solution to the Euthyphro problem is the same as the one proposed by Robert Merrihew Adams in *Finite and Infinite Goods* [Oxford: Oxford University Press, 1999], 35–6.)

gratifying to any agent, falling short of it may be frustrating, but these outcomes need not amount to getting things right or wrong, or doing better or worse. Even if considerations relevant to the aim have motivational force for any and every agent, their motivational force might be simply a push or a pull rather than a normative pro or con.

My answer to this objection is that having an aim already establishes a criterion of success or failure, which in turn yields a criterion of correctness for whatever can promote or hinder success.[24] Having an aim establishes a criterion of correctness in relation to that aim.

Yet the correctness defined by this criterion is relative to the aim, and the aim itself may not be correct. You may therefore ask me for a further justification, by asking, Why should I have the aim of intelligibility in behavior? Why should I seek to do what makes sense?

My reply to this demand is to say that the aim of self-understanding is inescapable for you, and in two senses. First, it is naturally inescapable for you as a human being. As a human being, you are naturally endowed with a theoretical intelligence, which is not a passive receiver of information but an active synthesizer, striving to make incoming information hang together so as to represent an intelligible world. You are also endowed with an objective self-awareness, a concept of yourself as a part of the world to be understood. These two endowments inevitably combine to yield the aim of understanding yourself, which inevitably motivates you to do what you can understand, whereupon you become a writer rather than a reader of your own behavior. In order to give up the aim of self-understanding, you would need either to omit yourself from your conception of the world, or to

---

[24] Why did I say, in note 22 above, that the criterion of correctness for belief cannot be fixed in similar fashion by belief's constitutive aim? The reason is that, when it comes to the constitutive aim of belief, we can demand a further justification – namely, a justification from the practical point of view.

give up thinking intelligently about that part of the world which is you. You can do such things temporarily, as I explained in Lecture 1, by losing yourself in an activity or in daydreams, for example, or simply by going to sleep. But you eventually come *to* – come to intelligent self-awareness, that is – and then you are back in the business of self-understanding again.

Because the aim of self-understanding is naturally inescapable, the question whether to have it is moot: you cannot help having this aim, like it or not. And because you have it, you engage in a kind of reasoning by which you end up writing your forthcoming behavior, with a warrant to write it as you like, without having to read it from evidence. The aim thereby sets you to reasoning in a way that makes you autonomous, constituting you as an agent, and the resultant behavior as action.

This brings me to the second sense in which the aim of self-understanding is inescapable: it is constitutively inescapable for you as an agent and hence as the kind of creature who can ask practical questions like "Why should I have this aim?" If this is indeed a practical question, posed in the spirit of deliberation between options, such as those of adopting or rejecting an aim, then it must be resolved via the sort of reasoning that is practical, in the sense that its resolution is authored rather than discovered, written rather than read. The question must therefore be resolved, I have argued, via reasoning that aims at self-understanding. To ask "why should I have the aim of making sense?" is to reveal that you already have it. If you don't seek to do what makes sense, then you are not in the business of practical reasoning, and so you cannot demand reasons for acting or aiming. Note that I am not yet holding out agency as a prize that you can attain by adopting its constitutive aim; indeed, I am not yet defending the aim of agency by means of any practical justification at all. Rather, I am pointing out that by demanding a reason for having the aim, you have demonstrated that you already have it, since if you didn't have it, you wouldn't be a subject of reasons, and so you wouldn't be asking for them. The grounds on which I rest this point are not practical; they are theoretical. They consist in my arguments for the conclusion that the aim of making sense is constitutive of agency.

$$* \quad * \quad *$$

The fact that you already have the aim constitutive of agency needn't blunt the force of your demand for a justification of it. Even if all of us share this aim, in our shared capacity as agents, you can still ask whether we ought to have it, and why.

To my ear, this question sounds like a demand for self-understanding. It asks: Is our convergence on this particular aim a fluke, or is there some underlying rationale? So interpreted, the question demands that the constitutive aim of action be justified in relation to the criterion set by the aim itself. Such a justification is easy to give; for as I have just explained, trying to do what makes sense, makes sense for creatures like us, who are by nature driven to understand the world and are aware of ourselves as especially salient parts of it.[25]

Of course, this justification is circular, and so it does not differentiate the aim of making sense from many other aims that are similarly self-justifying. Aims can justify themselves even though they are erroneous. You may therefore rephrase the present question so as to demand a justification from a standpoint outside the circle, so to speak. The fact that we agents have an aim in common, you may say, doesn't guarantee that we are not collectively misguided. How can we be sure that our agency doesn't implicate us in pursuing an erroneous aim?

---

[25] I also pointed out that there are occasions when trying to do what makes sense, makes no sense at all. On such occasions, the rational thing to do is to leave off being an agent for a while. I discuss this issue at length in "What Good Is a Will?," in *Action in Context*, ed. by Anton Leist (Berlin/New York: Walter de Gruyter/Mouton, 2007), 193–215.

But in relation to what criterion of correctness do you suspect intelligibility-seeking agency of error?[26] You may think that the ultimate criterion of correctness for action is something like "promoting the good," a criterion in relation to which aiming at intelligibility may well be erroneous. Unfortunately, this criterion is vacuous unless it is fleshed out by a substantive criterion of goodness. "The good" is by definition what it is correct to promote. We can of course aim at promoting what it is correct to promote, but we cannot do so without a substantive criterion.

Perhaps you think: There must be some substantively specifiable thing that it is in fact correct to promote, and aiming at intelligibility may be erroneous in relation to the aim of promoting that thing, whatever it is. If there is a fact of the matter as to what is good, then we would be wrong to aim at something else just in virtue of being agents.

But to raise this possibility is to give up on the purpose of the Kantian strategy. The purpose of the strategy is to explain the objectivity of practical thought without couching its demands in indicative judgments and positing states of affairs that make them true. If you assume that there already is a true criterion to which practical thought is answerable, then you have rejected the strategy as pointless before it begins. The Kantian strategy cannot justify its conception of practical reasoning in relation to some imagined true criterion, but that's not what it seeks or purports to do. The strategy begins by asking, "What if there is no such criterion?," and it tries to show that practical thought can be objective without one.

The Kantian argues that we need not worry about finding a criterion that's true,[27] because there is a criterion that's objective

---

[26] Here and below I echo arguments in Sharon Street's "Constructivism about Reasons."

[27] You might suspect that this disavowal of realism is disingenuous in my case. Haven't I identified what is to be promoted, objectively speaking – namely, one's own intelligibility? My version of the Kantian strategy may seem to

in another sense: it's objective in the sense of being inescapable, because it is fixed by an aim that is naturally inescapable for us as human beings and constitutively inescapable for us as agents. If you object that this aim may yet be erroneous in relation to the criterion that's true, then you are assuming away the normative void that the Kantian is trying to fill – assuming it away, I might add, without having anything substantive to fill it.

∗   ∗   ∗

The fact remains, however, that the only justification I have offered for the aim constitutive of agency is a circular justification, in relation to the criterion of correctness or aptness that is set by the aim itself. Aren't circular justifications always lame?

Here there is a risk of overestimating the similarity between foundational justifications in the practical and theoretical spheres. Circular justifications can be worrisome in the foundations of theoretical reasoning – for example, when we try to justify *modus ponens* as a rule of inference and find ourselves relying on *modus ponens* in the process.[28] But in that case, the aim of theoretical reasoning is not at issue: no question is being

---

have yielded a reductive realism, in which the concept of *the rational thing do,* for example, is reduced to the concept of *the intelligible thing to do.*

I have reasons for declining to make this claim. First, the intelligible thing to do is not the rational thing to do in any sense that would justify our being motivated to do it, since of course it owes its rationality to the role of that motive in constituting us as agents. Second, being the intelligible thing to do is an oddly indeterminate sort of property. What would be intelligible for someone to do depends on all of the ways in which he might reconceive of himself and his situation, including ways that would involve new concepts for personality types and interpersonal relations. Self-understanding, like all inquiry, allows for open-ended conceptual innovation, whose future course is not just unpredictable but indescribable from the perspective of the present.

[28] For discussion of these justifications, see Paul Boghossian, "How Are Objective Epistemic Reasons Possible?," *Philosophical Studies* 106 (2001): 340–80; and "Blind Reasoning," *Proceedings of the Aristotelian Society,* Supplementary Volume 77 (2003): 225–48. For the circularity objection in

raised about whether to aim at truth in our beliefs. The question is whether using a particular rule of inference is conducive to reaching the truth, and we are trying to reach the truth on this very question; but then we use the same rule whose truth-conduciveness is at issue, and we know that such pragmatically circular reasoning is not conducive to reaching the truth.

In this case, the aim of theoretical reasoning, true belief, provides a standard of success against which circular reasoning can be seen as a recipe for failure. This reasoning is clearly invalid, but it is invalid only in relation to what is unquestionably our aim in following it.

Our present question is very different. We are not trying to justify a particular rule of inference in relation to an unquestioned aim. Rather, we are asking whether and why we should have an aim that has been claimed to set the criterion of aptness or correctness that applies to practical reasoning. If you want to deprecate circular reasoning as invalid in this context, then you must be prepared to show that it is invalid in relation to some relevant criterion. You must show, in other words, that it is conducive to failure rather than success in relation to whatever criterion is applicable to justifying aims. If you propose a criterion different from the one that I have proposed, then you will already have rejected the claim currently at issue, that the latter is the relevant criterion. You will thus have begged the question. In relation to my proposed criterion, at least, a circular justification is not invalid, since to show that aiming at self-understanding is understandable is itself conducive to self-understanding.

Indeed, we can now see that if an aim sets the criterion of correctness for practical reasoning, then it cannot receive a noncircular

the practical case, see Stephen L. Darwall, "Autonomist Internalism and the Justification of Morals," *Nous* 24 (1990): 257–67.

justification, on pain of losing its criterion-setting status. For if it were justified in relation to some other criterion, then it could not in fact be what sets the criterion for practical reasoning: it would cede that status to the criterion in relation to which it had been justified. Thus, an aim that sets the criterion in relation to which aims are justified *must* not be justified except in relation to itself. And it cannot be faulted for lacking justification of a kind that it must not have.

You may now object that circular justifications are cheap: many different, incompatible aims can be justified in relation to themselves. What distinguishes any one such aim from the others?

What distinguishes one of them from the others, I say, is that it is constitutive of agency and therefore required to stand without a noncircular justification. That this aim is indeed constitutive of agency is not a practical matter to be established on practical grounds; it's a theoretical matter to be established in the philosophy of action. But once we have established that an aim is constitutive of agency, we must expect it to be solely self-justifying.

Now you ask, Couldn't our agency be constituted differently? And if so, why should we be constituted as agents in one way rather than another? As David Enoch has put it, Why be agents rather than *shmagents*? A *shmagent*, according to Enoch, is "a nonagent who is very similar to agents but who lacks the aim ... constitutive of agency."[29]

---

[29] "Agency, Shmagency: Why Normativity Won't Come from What Is Constitutive of Action," *Philosophical Review* 115 (2) (2006):169–98, p. 179. See also Peter Railton, "The Hypoethetical and Non-Hypothetical in Reasoning about Belief and Action"; and Luca Ferrero, "Constitutivism and the Inescapablity of Agency," in *Oxford Studies in Metaethics*, Vol. 4, ed. Russ Shafer-Landau (New York: Oxford University Press, forthcoming).

Insofar as an aim is naturally inescapable for us as human beings, however, giving it up is not possible in practice; and insofar as it accounts for the essential features of agency, giving it up while remaining "very similar to agents" is unlikely to be possible even in principle. We would have to exchange it for an alternative aim in virtue of which we would be something like autonomous (let's say *autonomish*) and would make something like choices (*shmoices*) among something like alternatives (*alternatoids*). Even if such a constitution were conceptually possible, I doubt whether we humans could embody it. The mere fact that we can modify words with comical prefixes and suffixes doesn't prove that we can somehow modify our agency.

But let me suppose for a moment that we could. I must then ask you to explain what you mean by the question "Why be agents rather than *shmagents?*" Are you contemplating agency and *shmagency* as alternatives between which you are trying to make an autonomous choice? Or are you viewing them as *alternatoids* between which you are trying to make an *autonomish shmoice?* If the former, then you are an agent, and the criterion for your choice is set by the aim constitutive of your agency; if the latter, then you are a *shmagent,* and the criterion for your *shmoice* is fixed by the *shaim* constitutive of your *shmagency.* If there are indeed alternative agential constitutions, the Kantian strategy doesn't take sides between them; it merely insists that questions must be asked and answered within the framework of some constitution.

No doubt, you will want to reply that you are speaking neither as agent nor as *shmagent*: you are holding both constitutions at arm's length and asking which one to adopt. But such detachment is impossible. In asking which constitution to adopt, you must be seeking guidance for *something* – a choice? a *shmoice?* some third thing? Until you specify what you want guidance for, you haven't posed a determinate question.

What the Kantian argues is that the criterion in relation to which guidance is possible must lie in the very nature of that which is to be guided. A question must establish criteria for what can count as a correct answer; if it fails to establish criteria for an answer, then it is not a fully constituted question. If "Why be an agent?" isn't about a choice or a *shmoice* or any third thing for which there is a criterion of correctness, then you aren't owed an answer, because you haven't yet asked a question.

* * *

Finally, you may wonder, What has become of the vaunted Kantian objectivity? The Kantian urged us to stop hoping for objective practical truths and settle for objectivity of some other kind; but we are now left with nothing but multiple constitutions, posing multiple questions. What kind of objectivity is that?

Calm down: we are not yet faced with multiple constitutions. I have been entertaining the possibility of *shmagency* in order to see what it might entail; no such alternative is on the horizon. Keep in mind that an alternative would have to account for *shmagential* phenomena corresponding to the agential phenomena explained by my account of agency. It would have to account for (something like) authorship of one's behavior from (something like) a deliberative stance, in which one sought to cope with (something like) an open future with the help of (something like) reasons, and so on. Otherwise, it would not constitute an alternative way of dealing with (anything like) practical matters, and so it would be no threat to the objectivity of practical thought.[30]

[30] There may indeed be variants of agency as I conceive it: I will describe one variant in Lecture 7. But these variants aren't sufficiently different from one another to alter the direction of rational progress, as I have called it, especially not in light of our need for mutual intelligibility in the service of joint improvisation. (Would *shmagents* do without self-understanding entirely? I doubt it.)

Even if there were such an alternative, it would not be relevant to the issue of objectivity, for reasons that I have already adduced. Neither agency nor *shmagency* can be objectively correct in itself. Asking whether agency rather than *shmagency* is objectively correct would be like asking whether a telephone is correct rather than a tree.[31] Agency or *shmagency* can be objectively correct *as* the solution to a determinate problem, or *as* the answer to a determinate question; but then the problem or question will invoke the criterion implicit in agency or the criterion implicit in *shmagency* (or some third criterion), by which one or the other can qualify as a correct solution or answer. The idea that there must be a correct criterion to invoke, and that its correctness must be objective in a sense that invokes no criterion whatsoever – *that* idea is nonsense, like the idea of objective correctness in a telephone or tree.[32]

Let's go back to the beginning of this lecture and see what progress we have made. We started with Bernard Williams's skepticism about the objectivity of reasons for acting, which led to a dilemma about practical reasoning, to the effect that it must be

---

[31] Or, as Sharon Street says, it would be like asking "Is the Empire State Building Taller?" ("Constructivism about Reasons," proof p. 225).

[32] You might think: That idea isn't nonsensical under a realist conception of practical thought, according to which a criterion of correctness for action can be *true*.

Really? If a criterion for action were true, it would then be objectively correct for us to *believe*, but only because truth is the criterion of correctness for belief. Indeed, what would be true, strictly speaking, would be our belief in the criterion, not the criterion itself; the criterion itself would just *be*. And as a criterion of correctness *for action*, it would be neither correct nor incorrect, except perhaps in relation to itself. It could not be correct in relation to no criterion whatsoever. Not even realism can deliver correctness in a criterion-less void.

either abortive or infinitely regressive. Have we managed to locate objective reasons for acting that do not set off an infinite regress of justifications?

I say that we have. We have found that action constitutively aims at making sense, by following considerations that render it intelligible. In relation to this aim, rendering an action intelligible amounts to justifying it, and so considerations in light of which an action makes sense amount to reasons for taking it.[33] The aim of making sense can itself be justified as making sense, but it cannot be given a noncircular justification, because it sets the ultimate criterion applied in practical reasoning, and so it cannot be justified in relation to any ulterior criterion. Although this aim cannot be justified practically without circularity, its criterion-setting status can be established by noncircular theoretical arguments, which show that it is indeed constitutive of agency and hence inescapable for us as creatures to whom reasons for acting apply.

Without this aim to make us susceptible to reasons, we would be incapable of acting for reasons, would not be agents, and would therefore be exempt from the force of reasons altogether. Our very ability to wonder whether to have this aim depends on our already having it. Hence reasons for acting depend for their influence on a motive, but it is not a motive dependent on our several subjective constitutions; it's a motive that provides our shared constitution as agents. Reasons are therefore objective,[34]

---

[33] Note that this claim does not invoke a principle of instrumental reasoning such as the Hypothetical Imperative. Rendering an action intelligible amounts to justifying it by showing it to be correct in relation to the standard established by the aim – a justification that doesn't depend on any practical principle mandating adoption of the means to achieving one's aims. Rather, the rationality of adopting means to one's aims depends on the intelligibility of doing so.

[34] As I explained in note 5, the objectivity at issue here is not the kind of objectivity discussed, for example, by Thomas Nagel in Chapter 10 of *The Possibility of Altruism*.

and their status as reasons can be established once and for all, by the philosophical analysis of agency. That's the Kantian strategy.

Williams concedes that this strategy is valid in principle. But he doubts whether it can establish the objective validity of moral norms. In his view, moral norms are not woven into the fabric of agency, any more than they are woven into the fabric of the world.[35] The most that will turn out to be objectively valid on such

---

[35] Allan Gibbard echoes this skepticism in his review of Korsgaard's Tanner Lectures ("Morality as Consistency in Living: Korsgaard's Tanner Lectures," *Ethics* 110 [1999]: 140–64. See also James Dreier, "Humean Doubts about the Practical Justification of Morality," in Cullity and Gaut (eds.), *Ethics and Practical Reason*, 81–99, p. 99: "Certain aspects of the Humean position deserve to be abandoned. We should abandon a hard-line metaphysical position according to which the very idea of practical reason is mysterious. Our skepticism should consist in doubts that the content of practical reason is anything like the content of morality.")

Gibbard advocates a view of normative discourse that, like Williams's internalism, seems to yield the dilemma that practical justifications must either go on forever or come to a merely contingent stop. As I have explained, Williams's internalism is the claim that every reason for acting must be able to engage some motive in the agent, so as to become the reason for which he acts. Gibbard's noncognitivism says that every normative claim expresses a motivational state of the speaker, which Gibbard calls the acceptance of a norm. Just as Williams's view appears to raise the question how to justify the motives that equip an agent to be influenced by reasons, Gibbard's view appears to raise the question how to justify the acceptance of norms. And the upshot of these questions appears to be the same in either case – namely, that justification must either go on forever or come to a merely contingent stop.

Gibbard does think that we apply the demands of morality to ourselves in an objective spirit, as applicable to us not only because we happen to self-apply them but also for the counterfactual circumstances in which we don't. But this mode of objectivity is not the mode asserted by Korsgaard.

(continued on page 148)

grounds, he thinks, are the requirements of logic and perhaps the Hypothetical Imperative, requiring the adoption of necessary means to intended ends. Nothing like Kant's Categorical Imperative, or any other moral requirement, will turn out to be inescapable for agents, in his view.

I share this negative expectation, that agency cannot be shown to depend on the acceptance of moral requirements.[36] Yet I don't agree that if agency doesn't require acceptance of the Categorical Imperative, then the most it can require is acceptance of logic plus the Hypothetical Imperative. I think that there is a middle ground between Williams and Kant.[37] The

For Gibbard, objectivity is a particular form in which demands or norms are couched. It is the form that includes the intensifier "whether you make this demand of yourself or not" – as in "Don't commit murder, whether you make this demand of yourself or not." For Korsgaard, objectivity is not a form of normativity; it is a philosophically demonstrable fact about particular norms – the fact that failing to apply them entails failing to qualify as a subject of norms.

[36] I am equally pessimistic about a variant of the Kantian strategy that Korsgaard has outlined more recently ("Realism and Constructivism in Twentieth-Century Moral Philosophy," in *Philosophy in America at the Turn of the Century* [Charlottesville: Philosophy Documentation Center, 2003], 99–122). Rather than formulate moral requirements that must be accepted by any agent, Korsgaard now proposes to formulate practical problems that must be faced by any agent – or, at least, by any agent who is subject to some general and immutable features of the human condition. The acceptance of moral requirements is then supposed to emerge as the unique solution to the problems that any human agent must face. This variant of the Kantian strategy does not attempt to show that practical reasoning must start from the acceptance of moral requirements; it attempts to show instead that practical reasoning must eventually arrive at the acceptance of moral requirements; but the strategies are similar in trying to show that moral requirements are inescapable for rational agents. I share the pessimism of Gibbard and Williams about the possibility of such a showing.

[37] Or, equivalently, between Gibbard and Korsgaard. See the two preceding footnotes.

middle ground is what I am inclined to call a Kinda Kantian strategy.

My Kinda Kantian strategy is to argue that the aim constitutive of agency can be seen to have pushed us in the direction of our moral way of life, and to be pushing us still in directions that are recognizably moral. The strategy thus provides a retrospective commentary on morality as a rational development, a form of rational progress.

In the modesty of its ambitions, this strategy resembles the philosophy of science.[38] Philosophers of science do not aspire to show that anyone seeking the truth empirically, by reasoning from observed phenomena, must inevitably arrive at Newton's laws of motion; rather, they show how the exigencies of theorizing about the phenomena favored adoption of Newton's theory – how theoretical reasoning about the actual world turned out to be pro-Newtonian. Just as reasoning in pursuit of the truth has been pro-Newtonian when applied to the phenomena of this world, I believe, so reasoning in pursuit of self-understanding has been pro-moral when applied to the human condition. In other words, practical reasoning has favored morality without requiring or guaranteeing it.

What is pro-moral about practical reasoning, conceived as the pursuit of self-understanding? In previous lectures I have offered several suggestions, which I will now summarize.

To begin with, I pointed out that practical reasoning, as I conceive it, encourages an agent to develop emotional and conative responses that can be understood as prompted by recognizable

---

[38] This view is described and rejected by John McDowell in "Virtue and Reason," in *Mind, Value, and Reality* (Cambridge, MA: Harvard University Press, 1998), 50–73, p. 50. See also Philip Pettit, "Substantive Moral Theory," *Social Philosophy and Policy* 25 (2008): 1–27.

kinds of things; and that it encourages him to avoid making an exception for himself as responding to things differently from everyone else. Practical reasoning thus favors developing intrapersonally coherent and interpersonally shared values.

I also argued that when rational agents interact, practical reasoning requires them to join in an improvisational collaboration, which is facilitated by adherence to socially shared scenarios. These scenarios are not scripted in advance by any individual author or group of authors; they are developed and continually revised by all performers in the course of repeated performances. And although the interests of individual performers may conflict with respect to potential revisions, there is a common interest in making the repertoire of scenarios more comprehensible, since it is a shared resource for self-understanding. In service of this interest, I argued, practical reasoning favors dispensing with dispensable distinctions between persons, a tendency reinforced by the rational pressure toward shared values.

I argued, further, that the improvisational collaboration that agents must form is generally facilitated by mutual understandings and hindered by deception. The rational incentive not to deceive is rarely strong enough to outweigh contingent motives in favor of deception, but it generates conflicts with those motives, and the conflicts are persistent enough to encourage the development of different values and scenarios, which do not favor deception, or do not favor it as strongly, so that they are compatible with outward as well as inward authenticity.

I also argued that recognizing one another as rational agents should inspire a complex interpersonal regard. We should see one another as fellow players, not just as the characters we play, and as jointly interested in proceeding together intelligibly in the former capacity, no matter how divergent our interests may be in the latter. We should see that each person is not just who he plays in real life but also the player within, whose self-presentation contributes to a collaborative enterprise that is essential to the exercise of his and everyone's rational agency. Finally, I argued that our participation in joint improvisation fosters the development of a discrete mental process that functions in various ways ordinarily associated with the conscience – arousing emotions of shame and guilt; holding us to our commitments; offering a self-regard that we seek to retain; and confirming that some courses of action are unthinkable.

These arguments suggest – no more than suggest – a rough configuration that our dealings together would acquire from practical reasoning in the very long run: shared values and scenarios, discouraging private exceptions, minimizing occasions for deception, shaped by an acknowledged common interest in comprehensibility, consequently free of unnecessary distinctions among persons, and supported by a psychic process recognizable as the conscience. This configuration would of course take further definition from the aspects of human nature that determine which ways of life we can authentically enact, so that we can genuinely understand ourselves in enacting them.

I think that we can see in this configuration some familiar features of morality: universality, transparency, mutuality. What we can't discern, from our philosophical perspective, is any particular moral principles or commandments or code. Where do these explicit expressions of morality come from? Let me conclude by briefly considering this question; it will then set the topic for my next lecture.

* * *

Where do moral principles come from? Well, social scenarios that have to be shared, and are developed under a pressure toward generality, will tend to strike compromises between the interests of players occupying different roles. Some players will consequently attempt to exploit these scenarios to personal advantage by making strategic departures from them. They will initiate the borrowing scenario, or the buying-and-selling scenario, and then bail out when the time comes for them to pay. They will appear to join in the question-and-answer scenario but then knowingly give false answers. Or they'll appear to join in the confider-and-confidant scenario but then violate a confider's confidence.

Understandably, people are then likely to develop a second-order scenario for policing adherence to the standard repertoire. There will be a scenario for dealing with cases in which joint improvisation has gone sour. This second-order scenario will include moves such as suspicion and accusation, rebuttal or admission, apology or restitution, making up or breaking up, and so forth.

Such a second-order scenario is likely to focus on precisely those aspects of the first-order scenarios where the latter pinch and where players are consequently tempted to slip out of them. And those contested aspects of the first-order scenarios are likely to include the marks they bear of the rational pressures toward universality and transparency, where the typical interests of those occupying particular roles will have been compromised for the sake of creating the most comprehensible basis for joint improvisation. The scenario of policing adherence to first-order scenarios is therefore likely to include explicitly moral moves, such as calling someone a cheater, accusing him of taking unfair advantage, or of discriminating against players of a particular kind. Such moves will be intelligible in the context of a scenario about disrupted first-order improvisations.

This second-order scenario can be neutral among the first-order scenarios that it supports. A single scenario for dealing with violated scenarios will serve equally for disputes between borrower and lender, buyer and seller, questioner and respondent, or confider and confidant. Indeed, these latter roles may be left behind upon ascent to the second order. To be sure, some first-order scenarios may contain subplots for untoward contingencies. Maybe the borrowing scenario already includes a branch for the contingencies of default and repossession. Still, the practice of borrowing must have its boundaries, the violation of which forces the participants out of character, so to speak, whereupon they are no longer borrower and lender but players coping with a failed improvisation.

The scenario for dealing with breakdowns in joint improvisation is likely to address not only deviations from particular first-order scenarios but also departures from the spirit in which self-enacting players must enter into joint improvisation itself. As I argued at the end of Lecture 3, even if players occupy roles that are unequal and mutually hostile, they are obliged to cooperate in order to attain the cognitive purpose for which they occupy such roles in the first place. Players will therefore have reason to require one another to recognize their fundamental equality and interdependence as co-improvisers. Those who violate the common understandings embodied in a particular scenario will be seen as showing a disregard for their fellow players, indicating that they cannot be counted on to play with others, as it were – that they are disposed to interact in ways that undercut rather than facilitate other people's ability to exercise their autonomy in concert with them. At such times, players will tend to resort to the second-order scenario for carrying out disputes among players.

Even in this case, they won't have fallen out of all characters entirely. They will rather have fallen into more generic characters, as players negotiating over the terms of their collaboration. This scenario represents a halfway house between social interaction and complete separation. A successful outcome will restore social relations, either through the resumption of the first-order scenario that has gone awry or simply through the restoration of a mutual willingness to interact. Failure in the second-order scenario leads to a rupture in relations, and not just between the players directly involved in the instant dispute. What is under discussion at the second order, after all, is the

fitness of one or both players to participate in joint improvisation – a matter that potentially interests all parties with whom
they might interact.

I suggest that the second-order scenario that I have roughly
described includes our practice of moral discourse. My suggestion implies that moral discourse is largely epiphenomenal on
morality itself.

As I see it, morality is distributed holographically throughout
our lives, in the various ways that our shared practices and values reflect various rational pressures and the underlying human
nature in light of which those pressures have been accommodated.[39] The marks of these rational pressures coalesce into a
coherent phenomenon only when viewed from certain angles
and in certain lights. One of those angles is salient from within
the scenario for negotiations between players. But that scenario is
not coextensive with moral discourse, since it also takes account
of improvisational infractions that are matters of etiquette or
friendship instead. And even in dealing with moral infractions,
it shouldn't be confused with morality itself, since it is merely a
scenario for moral discussion, not the source or grounds of what
is being discussed.

Indeed, I think that morality doesn't really exist, if by 'morality' is meant a single, coherent source of reasons, system of values, or deliberative perspective. The term 'morality' is rather an
interpretive label that we apply to a family of themes that run
through our way of life. The term is like 'art' or 'sport' or 'science', terms that name other families of practical themes, each

[39] Here I am in sympathy with Barbara Herman: "In an agent with a moral
character, the motive of duty is *dispersed* in the motives that satisfy the constraints of the deliberative field" (*Moral Literacy* [Cambridge, MA: Harvard
University Press, 2007], 21).

held together by no more than internal family resemblances. Of course, we can theorize about questions such as "What is art?" or "What is sport?" or "What is science?," but such theorizing is never more than an attempt to find interpretively fruitful ways of teasing out and braiding up various themes that run through our lives. We do make statements of the form "Science tells us ..." or "Art shows us ...," but philosophers who set out to find the one true wellspring of Science's findings or Art's revelations are likely to search in vain.

Yet when people say "Morality requires ...," philosophers feel confident of finding a single wellspring of moral requirements – a particular principle or value or method or perspective from which the requirements of morality draw their content and authority. There is no such thing, in my view. There is indeed a perspective from which moral requirements are articulated: it's the perspective of a socially shared scenario for policing adherence to especially demanding aspects of our joint improvisations. But the requirements of morality don't originate in this perspective or derive their authority from it. It is merely the forum in which they are abstracted from the specific values and practices where the true authority lies.

I am skeptical about the importance of moral judgment in guiding our conduct. Support for this skepticism can be found in the testimony of people who perform heroic acts of morality – the sort of acts that ought to have what Kant called moral worth, if anything does. People who saved Jews from the Holocaust, for example, often disappointed postwar interviewers who asked about their reasoning and motives.

These moral heroes would say things like "They appeared at my door, and I didn't have it in me to turn them away," "They needed help, and I couldn't refuse," "It was the obvious thing to do," often failing to invoke any moral concepts such as obligation or virtue.[40] Seeing needy victims, they found themselves constrained to help, but what constrained them was not any particular thought about morality; it was rather their whole selves – that is, their entire self-conceptions – which would have made refusal unintelligible coming from them. The obviousness of helping, the unintelligibility of refusing, were woven into who they were and how they lived, not articulated in occurrent moral judgments.

I am not saying that these heroes helped others in need simply because doing so made sense, or that their seemingly moral

---

[40] See, e.g., Marek Halter, *Stories of Deliverance: Speaking with Men and Women Who Rescued Jews from the Holocaust*, trans. Michael Bernard (Chicago: Open Court, 1998); Samuel P. Oliner and Pearl M. Oliner, *The Altruistic Personality: Rescuers of Jews in Nazi Europe* (New York: The Free Press, 1988); Gay Block and Malka Drucker, *Rescuers: Portraits of Moral Courage in the Holocaust* (New York: Holmes & Meier, 1992); and Pearl M. Oliner, *Saving the Forsaken: Religious Culture and the Rescue of Jews in Nazi Europe* (New Haven, CT: Yale University Press, 2004). One of the most common explanations offered by rescuers was simply this: "It was the normal thing to do." Here are some relevant quotations: "To give a hand to someone who needs help? [...] But ... that's only normal!" (Halter, p. 5); "I thought it was something quite natural. We knew we must help these people. It is not even pity, it's normal, that's all" (Halter, p. 35; see also pp. 52, 158, 238, 291; Gay and Drucker, p. 9; Oliner, pp. 50, 88); "I think I reacted spontaneously, because I am like that" (Halter, p. 51); "You see a child, you see how, ... in the street, in the station, everything is refused, everything except death – and in the early morning light this child looks at you with his big eyes, with enormous eyes: what do you do? I did it, that's all" (Halter, p. 74); "I never spent my time asking why I did all that. I did it, that's all" (Halter, p. 109; see also p. 80); "[In response to the question 'Why did you decide to help?'] I decided nothing. A man knocked on my door. He said he was in danger. I asked him to stay, and he stayed till the end of the war" (Halter, p. 108); "I cannot give you any reasons. It was not a question of reasoning. Let's put it this way. There were people in need and we helped them....People always ask how we started, but we didn't start. It started. And it started very gradually. We never gave it much thought" (Oliner and Oliner, p. 216); "I don't know exactly why I helped. It's just the kind of person I am" (Block and Drucker, p. 232).

concern was really a concern for their own intelligibility. Their reasons for helping others were the substantive concerns in light of which helping made sense – their sympathy for other human beings, their sense of being equally vulnerable "but for the grace of God," their engagement in practices of reciprocity, so on. Their actions authentically manifested such concerns, not just their conception of what would make sense in light of them.

Intelligibility is merely a higher-order aim that would have shaped those substantive concerns. Its being a higher-order aim does not entail that it was of greater importance or influence in the people's lives; on the contrary, it was of minor importance and influence – minor but also persistent and pervasive. What it would have imparted to their more important and influential concerns is an overall moral configuration, which might have been reflected in their moral discourse but was not determined by it.

My picture of morality thus raises doubts about the way metaethics is generally practiced, via the analysis of moral discourse and judgment. We do say things such as "Lying is wrong," but this remark is epiphenomenal on the way of life in which our practices of communication are embodied. Analyzing the semantics, metaphysics, and epistemology of "Lying is wrong" will reveal very little about the fundamental nature of morality.

I just said that moral discourse is largely epiphenomenal on morality. If it were entirely epiphenomenal, it would make no practical difference; it would be nothing but idle commentary. I do think that it makes a practical difference, though, and so I need to explain the difference it makes. Specifically, I need to explain why resorting to the second-order scenario of moral discourse makes any difference in the way we behave.

This second-order scenario affects our behavior, I think, by highlighting our dependence on others to collaborate with us in joint improvisation. If I say, "You owe me ten dollars," I am still enacting the lending scenario, by speaking in my capacity as a creditor trying to collect. What's at stake is your credit rating, which is a feature of the lending scenario. But if I say, "You cheated me," I have dropped the character of lender and resorted to the character of a player in social scenarios, speaking to another player who has proved unreliable onstage. Now much more is at stake. It's one thing to prove unreliable as a borrower; it's quite another thing to prove unreliable as a player in social scenarios. The first affects only your eligibility for loans; the second affects your eligibility for social interaction altogether.

As I explained in Lecture 4, anxiety about one's eligibility for joint improvisation can constitute either of two moral emotions: shame or guilt. Moral discourse belongs to a scenario in which we point out and discuss improvisational defaults of a sort that arouse these emotions, which are aversive and which therefore motivate us to avoid whatever occasions them, if possible. That's why moral discourse is not entirely epiphenomenal on the moral patterns in our way of life. Even so, I think that it is a sideshow to the main action of morality.

6

Theory

I say that practical reasoning is an experimental discipline.
The process of figuring out how we can enact intelligible and
authentic versions of ourselves cannot be boiled down to a syllogism. It cannot be formalized in a calculus of "practitions,"[1]
means and ends, or desires and beliefs. We reason practically, in
the long run, by continually trying out clearer, more coherent,
and yet more ingenuous ways of being and doing; and there is
no substitute for trying them out, which is a process of trial and
error.

Several reasons have emerged for the necessity of experimentation. One reason is the radical holism of self-understanding,
which involves a complex web of explanatory connections, such
as these:

- What it will ultimately make sense to do depends on what it
  makes sense to value, but what it makes sense to value can
  depend on what it would consequently make sense to do.
- There are many ways of valuing things, and each must be
  understood in light of the rest, because they are mutually
  reinforcing or inhibiting.

[1] See, e.g., Hector-Neri Castañeda, "Practical Thinking, Reasons for
Doing, and Intentional Action: The Thinking of Doing and the Doing of
Thinking," *Philosophical Perspectives* 4 (1990): 273–308.

- Having understandable ways of replying to other people can depend on understanding their replies to oneself, which can depend in turn on having made oneself understood to them.
- People therefore tend to converge on particular ways of acting that are understandable as the ways people act in order to be understandable in just those ways.
- They make this shared way of life more intelligible by coordinating it with shared evaluative responses that follow the contours of recognizable kinds and avoid unnecessary exceptions.

Faced with this multiply interconnected web of explanatory factors, people must simply take hold of their lives and start tweaking.

Another reason for the necessity of experimentation is the ever-present possibility of acquiring new ways of valuing and acting through habituation. In order to figure out whether one can honestly be a spouse, an expatriate, a fan of hip-hop, courageous, politically active, artistically inclined, one may have to try on the envisioned character and see whether one can make it one's own. This process may involve an initial period of inauthentic pretense, during which one gives oneself a chance to cultivate the values and tastes that one would need in order to play the character for real.[2] The outcome of these experiments in living is often difficult to predict.

Yet a third reason for the necessity of experimentation is the role of human nature in constraining the parts that one can play authentically. A way of life that would be a more comprehensible variation on one's own might nevertheless be ruled out

---

[2] I discuss this phenomenon in "Motivation by Ideal," *Philosophical Explorations* 5 (2002) 89–104; reprinted in *Self to Self* (New York: Cambridge University Press, 2006), 312–29.

by the fact that people cannot rationally live that way, because they cannot live that way without inauthenticity, which entails self-misunderstanding. Think of the utopian communities that required more self-denial than people can maintain. Until people tried living that way, no one knew whether it would work.

I think that we are severely limited in our ability to anticipate the outcome of practical reasoning in the long run. We may be able to frame plausible hypotheses about specific features that are likely to appear in any workable way of life, but many features of human life are revisable. Thus, attempting to predict or dictate the overall outcome of practical reasoning would be like attempting to predict or dictate the outcome of scientific inquiry. The main thing that philosophers can do, and what I have tried to do, is to identify some rational pressures whose influence should be detectable over time, and to explain why those pressures favor ways of life structured by universality, transparency, and mutuality, with an inner pair of eyes for reinforcing that structure and social practices for policing it. That's as far as philosophy can go, in my view.

I have also argued that the universality, transparency, and mutuality favored by practical reasoning do not add up to a unified source of reasons, point of view, or system of thought such as philosophers have in mind when they speak of morality. Morality, in my view, is a family of themes that emerge from the endless variations jointly played by self-enacting agents. Why, then, have philosophers spent so much effort and ink on systematic moral theories? Why propound a Principle of Utility or a Categorical Imperative if morality is holographically distributed throughout our way of life, and our way of life evolves through trial and error?

I think that there is a role for systematic moral theory to play, but it isn't the role that its exponents envision. Explaining this

role – and in particular, how it is played by the two principles
just mentioned – is the task that I've set for this lecture.

First, however, I want to consider the null hypothesis of moral
theory – namely, moral relativism. According to moral relativism, no moral system can be uniquely correct, since incompatible
systems are equally viable, and what's correct is always relative to
some such system. My view of practical reason accounts for some
of the phenomena that make moral relativism tempting, and yet
it doesn't ultimately succumb to the temptation. It explains the
considerable degree of contingency in morality without conced-
ing that anything goes.

$$* \quad * \quad *$$

The degree of contingency results from the gradualist, trial-
and-error method by which ways of life evolve.[3] People start with
the way of life that they have – their existing repertoire of roles,
values, and scenarios – and they gradually work to simplify and
unify that way of life, while enhancing the resources it offers
for authentic self-enactment. Even if every society started out
with the same hunting-and-gathering way of life, different societies would gravitate in different directions, especially if their
physical circumstances differed. One wouldn't expect all improvisational theater troupes to end up with exactly the same repertoire, either.

Nevertheless, all societies and all individuals develop their
improvisational material under the same rational pressures
and some of the same empirical constraints as well. Insofar as
there is a fixed human nature that is common to members of
the species, all will seek roles and scenarios that can be enacted
by creatures with that nature, and enacted by such creatures

---

[3] Here I will use the phrase 'way of life' to encompass not only practical scenarios but also the roles played and the values held by characters within
them.

authentically. They will also develop this material under the same rational pressure toward comprehensibility, which is an objective feature of practical reasoning.[4]

Insofar as all societies are solving similar improvisational problems under similar rational pressures and empirical constraints, their ways of life will be roughly assessable as better or worse, as more or less advanced, on a scale that is not itself peculiar to any one society. There really is such a thing as objective progress, because there is a substantive criterion of success in practical reasoning, which provides an objective aim for the development of any improvisational resources whatsoever. But we should also expect a large degree of rationally contingent variation, because very different ways of acting and reacting may be equally intelligible and authentic. Different improvisational repertoires can provide human beings with similar scope for making sense of themselves.

What's more, we should expect to find in some cases that one way of life is rationally inaccessible from another, in that it cannot intelligibly be adopted by people already inhabiting the other way of life. Borrowings from the former way of life may simply make no sense within the repertoire of self-understandings available in the latter. Thus, we should not be surprised to find intractable disagreements about how to live, cultural distances that cannot rationally be bridged. We may even find unbridgeable distances between ways of life that can be ranked as objectively more and less rational, leaving the latter as rational dead ends, from within which there is no intelligible way of making progress.[5]

---

[4] As I will explain in Lecture 7, I think that there are actually rational pressures toward two different kinds of comprehensibility, expressed in causal-psychological explanation, on the one hand, and narrative, on the other. My suggestion that the pressures toward comprehensibility are universal must therefore be qualified, insofar as the relative strength of the pressures toward these distinct cognitive goals can vary across people and societies.

[5] I discussed similar "dead ends" on the individual level in Lecture 1.

Many of these phenomena – rationally contingent variation, intractable disagreements, developmental dead ends – are the typical starting points for philosophical arguments that lead to moral relativism. They are claimed to indicate a lack of objective standards by which to rank divergent moral codes, or even to rank morality over immorality. But these phenomena are compatible with objectivity in the overall trend or direction of practical reason, the trend toward participation in an increasingly comprehensible way of life. I conclude that they aren't really evidence for relativism at the most fundamental level.

Let me turn, then, to positive normative theories. My view of such theories is that they are idealizations whose value is to highlight the moral family of themes in our way of life. These idealizations are comparable to the ideal gases or ideal surfaces imagined in scientific theory.

As we know, there are no frictionless surfaces or extensionless particles in nature, but imagining such things enables us to simplify and clarify our calculations about the things that there are. The resulting calculations are accurate enough, but not just that; they are also more perspicuous than more accurate calculations would be. They show the perfectly lawlike behavior that real objects only approximate, because the laws hold only *ceteris paribus* – other things being equal – and other things are never really equal in nature. By prescinding from those messy "other things," our idealizations make the phenomena more comprehensible, providing more elegant generalizations with which to "grasp together," not the actual phenomena, but something else that is close enough.

Note that I am speaking here of idealizations in an intellectual sense of the term. The frictionless surfaces and point-particles imagined in physics are ideal for the purpose of understanding physical phenomena, not because their existence would make the world a better place. Idealizations are cognitively ideal, because they reveal simple patterns in complexity, rendering the actual phenomena more intelligible.

As vehicles of understanding, idealizations can figure in our self-understanding and hence in our practical reasoning. And among the aspects of ourselves that idealizations can help us to understand are the very methods by which we collectively achieve self-understanding, and in particular, the ways in which those methods induce moral patterns and themes into our way of life. That's the role of normative theories, as I conceive them. Let me explain how the foremost such theories play this role.

My metaethics is most hospitable to Kantian moral theory: no surprise there. In fact, I think that my metaethics helps to explain why Kant's Categorical Imperative works in practical application. I'll start by explaining briefly how the Imperative works according to Kant, as I interpret him; then I will turn to its role as an idealization in our self-understanding.[6]

Kant thinks that the Categorical Imperative, which expresses the content of our duty, can be derived from the very concept of a duty. The concept of a duty, he thinks, is the concept of an objectively authoritative practical requirement. Just figure out how anything can be objectively required of us, Kant says, and you will find that there can be only one thing that is so required, and it will be what we are morally required to do.

To represent objectivity in the practical realm, Kant uses the concept of a *law*, but I think that the concept of law is already too much like the concept of duty to be helpful in this context.

---

[6] The following interpretation of Kant is based on "The Voice of Conscience," *Proceedings of the Aristotelian Society* 99 (1999): 57–76, reprinted in *Self to Self*, 110–28; and "A Brief Introduction to Kantian Ethics," also in *Self to Self*, 16–44.

Kant's conception of practical objectivity is better expressed, I believe, by the concept of common knowledge.[7] A judgment is objective in this sense when it is what anyone would think, and anyone would think that anyone would think, and so on, like the judgment that 2 plus 2 equals 4, which anyone can see to be not just true but obviously true in a way that anyone can see. Kant imagines rational agents as occupying a shared intellectual space in which various matters are publicly visible, so that everyone sees them and sees their being seen by everyone else.[8]

The practical matters that are common knowledge among rational agents, according to Kant, have to do with which considerations count as good reasons for which actions. The considerations themselves will of course be knowable only by particular agents, and the actions will be available only to particular agents as well. What Kant imagines to be publicly visible in the imaginary space shared by all rational agents is which considerations count as good reasons for which actions.

Consider an example. Subjectively, not wanting to part with money seems like a good reason to default on a loan; but if it was objectively a good reason, then anyone should be able to see that it was a good reason, and to see that anyone could see it, and so on. The judgment that it was a good reason would be like the

---

[7] A related interpretation of Kant, extending well beyond his moral theory, is being pursued independently by Timothy Rosenkoetter, in as-yet-unpublished work.

[8] I will not distinguish between public accessibility and common knowledge, although they are not exactly the same: what is in public view may not be common knowledge if some members of the public fail to *look*. The difference is less stark in the Kantian conception of public accessibility, in which access is afforded to all subjects through individual reflection or intuition. What is accessible to a subject by these means is already known latently or implicitly, in the sense that it would be known explicitly if only the subject thought about it. What everyone *would* judge if he considered the matter, and would judge that everyone *would* judge if he considered the matter, can therefore be latent common knowledge.

judgment that 2 plus 2 equals 4, clear to all judges, and clearly so. Thus, if thrift were an objectively good reason for defaulting on a loan, then its being a good reason would be common knowledge among all practical thinkers.

If a practical judgment is objective in this sense, then it has authority because it is *unappealable*. Imagine, for example, that thrift really is an objectively good reason to default on a loan. In that case, there is no practical perspective from which it will be judged otherwise, because its being a good reason to default will be evident to anyone, no matter what his perspective. Someone who arrives at this judgment will consequently find that reconsidering it from another point of view will make no difference, since the judgment will be confirmed from whatever point of view he considers it. To borrow a phrase from Harry Frankfurt, the judgment that thrift is a good reason to default will then resound through all levels of possible reconsideration.[9] What's more, this resounding authority will be audible to anyone who considers what to do with a loan, since "Thrift is a good reason to default" will be not only what he thinks but also what he thinks anyone would think, and would think that anyone would think – including himself, should he reconsider. When he judges in favor of defaulting on grounds of thrift, he will simultaneously imagine a chorus of affirming judgments from all other practical perspectives, just as he can imagine everyone agreeing with his judgment that 2 plus 2 equals 4. In making this judgment, he speaks to himself with the resounding voice of authority – or, rather, he does if thrift is indeed an objectively good reason for defaulting.

When an agent makes an objective practical judgment, in other words, he recognizes that there is no getting around it,

---

9 Harry Frankfurt, "Freedom of the Will and the Concept of a Person," in *The Importance of What We Care About* (Cambridge: Cambridge University Press, 1987), 11–25, p. 21; "Identification and Wholeheartedness," in *ibid.*, 159–76, p. 168.

because there is no practical perspective from which it can be reversed. Having no prospect of successful appeal, he has no rational alternative but to accept the judgment, and seeing that there is no alternative is what motivates his obedience. His obedience can then be described as motivated by respect for the judgment's authority.

✳　✳　✳

Of course, thrift is not an objectively good reason to default on a loan. It couldn't be. For if it were an objectively good reason, then the thought that anyone (including any borrower) would think it a good reason would be a thought that anyone (including any prospective lender) would think, and so no one would lend anything in the first place. The notional public space shared by rational agents would afford this view of the matter to potential borrowers only if it also afforded the same view to potential lenders, along with the view of its being seen by potential borrowers. Potential lenders would therefore be deterred from lending.

Moreover, the thought that thrift cannot be an objectively good reason to default is itself an objective practical judgment, publicly visible in the same notional space. Anyone can see, and anyone can see that anyone can see, that there would be no loans at all if everyone saw thrift as a good reason to default on them.

The last two paragraphs are my reconstruction of Kant's proof that the maxim of saving money by defaulting on loans involves what he calls a contradiction in conception, and hence that it violates the Categorical Imperative.[10] Now, if the conclusion of this proof were that thrift's *not* being a good reason to default was objective, then the proof would stand as a decisive

---

[10] "Contradiction in conception" may not be an apt description of such cases, but that's what Kant calls them. (See the following note and its accompanying text.)

argument against defaulting from thrift. Unfortunately, what the proof establishes is, not that thrift is *objectively not* a good reason, but that it is *not objectively* a good reason – that its being a good reason to default cannot be objective. And *that* is why Kant's *Groundwork* runs to three parts. The third part is needed to explain why we are debarred from acting on what cannot be objectively good reasons; it's needed, that is, to explain why we are required to act for reasons whose validity can be objective.

In Kant's mouth, what I have just said comes out sounding like this. When I say that the validity of thrift as a reason to default could not be common knowledge, Kant says that the maxim of defaulting from thrift could not be a universal law. When I say that we are required to act on reasons whose validity could be objective, Kant says that we are required to act on a maxim that could be a universal law. Actually, he says that we are required to act on a maxim that we could *will* to be universal law; I'll explain that twist in a moment. In my terminology, the twist yields the requirement to act for reasons that we could will to be objectively valid. This requirement is of course the Categorical Imperative itself, in its first formulation.

How could we be required to act for reasons that we could will to be objectively valid? I don't think that Kant can answer this question successfully, but he does try. His attempt depends on a theory of autonomous action.

In order to act autonomously, we cannot simply behave at random: autonomous action must be nonrandom in some sense. One way for our behavior to be nonrandom would be for it to result from efficient causes; but its being the effect of causes would entail that it still wasn't autonomous, or so Kant believes. Fortunately, there is another way for us to behave nonrandomly – namely, by behaving in accordance with some piece of practical guidance, such as the specification of a reason for acting. Of course, behaving in accordance with practical guidance can't simply be a matter of falling under its causal influence, else this case of nonrandom behavior would collapse into the previous one, in which autonomy is excluded by efficient causation. Following practical guidance must therefore be a matter, not of registering its effects, but of deferring to its authority, which in Kant's view is not just a causal matter. As I have explained, we regard practical guidance as authoritative when we regard it as objective – that is, as common knowledge among practical thinkers. We follow such guidance because we see it to be unappealable, impossible to evade. In order to act autonomously, then, we must follow some piece of practical guidance, such as a reason for acting, because we see that there is no getting around it. Autonomy thus depends on the perception of objectively valid reasons.

This conception of autonomy raises two problems, whose solution ultimately leads to the final formulation of the Categorical Imperative. One problem is that we rarely find reasons for acting that are authoritative in the requisite sense. The beauty of a BMW may strike us as a good reason to buy one; but is it obviously a good reason, in a way that anyone would see and would see that anyone would see? Hardly. Thrift may strike us as a good reason to forego buying a BMW; but would anyone think so, and think that anyone would think so? Not clear. Most reasons for acting seem easy to get around, and so they seem not to be authoritative in the sense represented by Kant with the notion of universal law. (There are exceptional cases in which we do find reasons that are authoritative in this sense; I'll discuss them in a moment, after discussing the problem of their scarcity.)

Kant thinks that this problem will yield to a solution, which happens to be needed in any case to deal with another, deeper problem. The deeper problem is this. Suppose that there were no getting around some reason for acting because it was like an obstacle that we simply encountered blocking our path, albeit in that notional space that we share with all rational agents. In that case, Kant believes, our taking guidance from it would not be autonomous, since that guidance would have been imposed on us, as if from the outside. Kant concludes that in order to act autonomously, we need to act, not for reasons that we *find* to be authoritative, but for reasons that we *will* to be authoritative: there has to be no getting around them, but only because we will there to be none. Autonomous action must be done, in other words, out of respect for reasons that *we endow* with authority. And if we can thereby endow a reason with authority, then our not having found it to be authoritative is no longer a problem, either. We can choose to regard the beauty of a BMW as an authoritative reason for buying one, and not to regard thrift as an authoritative reason against, thereby reaching an autonomous decision to buy a new car. Both problems of autonomy are thus solved at once.

Legitimate questions can be raised as to whether we really can will a reason for acting to be authoritative. But in the third part of the *Groundwork*, Kant argues that, whether or not we really can do so in fact, we must act on the assumption that we can, because we must act on the assumption that we are acting autonomously. We must therefore think that we are following a piece of practical guidance that is authoritative because we will it to be so. Or, in Kant's language, we must assume that we are acting on a maxim that we have willed to be universal law.

Now, if a reason for acting is such that we could not possibly will it to be authoritative, then we cannot coherently think that we are following its guidance autonomously. In that case, the necessity of acting on the assumption that we are acting autonomously makes it impossible for us to follow its guidance without contradicting ourselves.[11] Hence the necessity of acting only on a maxim that we can will to be universal law: the derivation of the Categorical Imperative is complete. I cannot will that thrift count as an authoritative reason for defaulting on a

[11] So maybe Kant's talk of contradictions is appropriate, after all. See the preceding note.

loan, since willing it to be authoritative would entail willing that its validity be common knowledge among all practical thinkers, tipping off all potential creditors to the reasons that would lead their potential debtors to default, and thereby wiping out the availability of the very credit that I am proposing to abuse. Since willing this reason to be authoritative would thus be obviously self-defeating, I can't think of myself as willing it to be authoritative while acting upon it, and so I cannot think of myself as acting on the reason autonomously. But I have to think of myself as acting for reasons autonomously. And that's why my proposed default fails the test of the Categorical Imperative.

∗ ∗ ∗

Having asked you to consider this derivation of the Categorical Imperative, I am tempted to repeat a quip of Elizabeth Anscombe's:[12]

> I say 'Consider this' really with a view to saying 'let us not consider it here'. It is too complicated.

Yes, it *is* too complicated, Kant's derivation, but I am not asking you to dwell on the complications. I have presented the derivation only for the sake of demonstrating that it can indeed be presented in the terms that I have substituted for Kant's – specifically, in terms of objective authority understood as common knowledge among practical thinkers.

Even in my formulation, of course, Kant's derivation of the Categorical Imperative is based on a conception of rational agency that differs significantly from mine. Why then do I think that it works in practice? It works, I believe, as a useful idealization of social interaction among self-enacting improvisers – that is, among rational agents.

---

[12] *Intention* (Cambridge, MA: Harvard University Press, 2000), p. 20.

In my first three lectures, I explored how the rational agent's project of self-understanding can best be carried out, given that he must interact with other agents engaged in the same project. I compared these interactions to the joint improvisations of actors ingenuously playing themselves, by doing what would make sense coming from people like them under circumstances like theirs. I pointed out that each improviser is under some rational pressure to arrive at an identity that he can attribute to himself, project to others, and assume that they attribute to him, so that a single, shared conception of him can figure in the explanation of everyone's behavior. I pointed out further that the best way for each improviser to find intelligible ways of interacting with others is to participate in socially shared scenarios, in which a limited selection of moves and countermoves, with their standard explanations, is made available to all parties. I also pointed out that violations of these scenarios are likely to give rise to complaints along moral lines, because they focus on aspects of the scenarios that facilitate consensus and generality at the expense of some participants' private interests. Finally, I pointed out that the personal values suitable for inclusion in socially negotiated identities are likely to be supportive of morality, for similar reasons.

All of these points suggest that the key to interacting rationally with other rational agents is to act on understandings that are or could be common knowledge. When everyone knows, and knows that everyone knows, who we are and how we do things, each of us will be most likely to find improvisational possibilities that make sense to pursue and that will lead to other intelligible possibilities. Relying on common understandings about ourselves and our ways of doing things is the best way of getting on with self-enacting improvisation in concert with other self-enacting improvisers; it is, in the phrase of my title, how we get along.

✷ ✷ ✷

This aspect of joint improvisation is represented in theories of improvisational theater by the notion of the *frame*.[13] Successful improvisation requires all of the players to make moves that are intelligible within a single, shared frame – that is, a single, gradually accumulating body of common knowledge about who their characters are and how those characters are motivated.

At the beginning of an improvisation, the frame is empty: there is no fact of the matter as to the time, place, circumstances, and *dramatis personae* of what is to follow. As soon as a player does or says something, he inserts information into the frame – not just the information that someone has done or said that thing, but also whatever information is implied or presupposed by what has been done or said. If one player opens the scene by saying to another, "Doctor, I can't sleep at night," then he has established that he is a patient consulting a doctor about his insomnia. That information is now part of the frame.

At this point, the second player must not say, "I'm not your doctor; I'm your dog" – or anything else that would be incompatible with what has already been entered into the frame. Doing so would render the frame incoherent and hence unusable as a basis for further improvisation. The second player must respond in a way that is consistent with the frame and preserves its ongoing extensibility. His response will then establish further fictional truths on the basis of which the subsequent action can proceed.

Because one and the same frame constrains all the players and receives contributions from all of them, it is usually imagined as a publicly accessible object, existing outside the mind of any particular player. It is like a central game board on which

---

[13] See, e.g., R. Keith Sawyer, *Improvised Dialogues: Emergence and Creativity in Conversation* (Westport, CA: Ablex Publishing, 2003). Sawyer argues that the "frame" is an emergent property of an improvisation, not reducible to attitudes or interactions of the individual players.

players make moves that advance the state of play, in the open for all to see.

When an improvisation begins, it may follow an existing scenario in the players' repertoire, or it may take a previously unexplored course. If a known scenario is initiated, subsequent actions and utterances may either stick to it or strike out in new directions. Given the process by which the troupe's repertoire evolves, however, each innovation will amount to an ad lib proposal for alterations of or additions to the existing corpus of scenarios. Novel moves will lay down new paths that could in principle be retraced in future performances, if they prove dramatically fruitful.

This additional function of novel moves may not constrain the possibilities for innovation among theatrical improvisers, whose scenarios are fictional. But it may make a significant difference among rational agents developing scenarios whose performance is meant to be authentic.

Suppose that one player strikes out in a novel direction by asking another for a loan. (The borrowing-and-lending scenario is not yet in the repertoire.) If this player is in the theater, he can be introducing this theme into the repertoire whether he intends for his character to repay the loan or to default. The bad-loan scenario would be a perfectly viable addition to the repertoire. In subsequent performances, the player who is asked for a loan will know that his interlocutor may be initiating a scenario that has two possible endings, and he will be prepared to play along with either one. But he will be prepared to play along with either version of the scenario only because he doesn't have to play the part authentically, expressing his actual motives toward a real transaction. If he had to play the part for real, he would never agree to begin the loan scenario in the first place, if the bad-loan ending were part of the common repertoire.

For this reason, requesting a loan while intending to default cannot initiate a viable addition to the repertoire of real life, because it cannot belong to a shared scenario whose dramatic premises are common knowledge. The bad-loan version of the scenario can have a first performance; it can have innumerably many first performances, among different players. But it can never be initiated as a proposed addition to the repertoire of scenarios on which the joint improvisations of rational agents depend.

In Kant's mouth, what I have just said comes out sounding like this. The dishonest borrower could not introduce his maxim as legislation for the Kingdom of Ends – legislation, presumably, about what counts as a good reason for what. In Kant's theory, the Kingdom of Ends is an imaginary commonwealth in which each citizen contributes the maxims of his actions as pieces of legislation for all, thereby willing them to be universal law – or, in my terminology, common knowledge. The constraints on maxims thus entered into law are formally similar to the constraints on improvisational initiatives, considered as contributions to the repertoire of shared scenarios, which have to be common knowledge in order to serve their purpose.

Not surprisingly, the improvisational initiatives that could not be proposed as innovations to the repertoire will tend to be the ones that would never be accepted by all parties as a basis for joint improvisation, and would therefore have to be somehow concealed or falsified by anyone trying to act on them, who would thereby defeat their purpose as scenarios. The pressure emanating from the need to improvise with others is therefore like the requirement to act on maxims that could serve as laws for the Kingdom of Ends. And that is why Kant's moral theory can serve as an idealization for the interactions among rational agents.

If the Categorical Imperative really can serve as an idealization of the key desideratum for joint improvisation, then it can serve that function normatively and not just descriptively. Precisely because it provides a model of how rational agents interact, it renders that way of interacting intelligible, thereby recommending it in the manner of reasons recommending action, by showing that it makes sense. We can sometimes understand ourselves by imagining that we are practical legislators, laying down laws about which actions make sense in which circumstances. This idealization will be especially useful when we are tempted to make exceptions for ourselves or to open a second set of books on ourselves. These possibilities appear suspect, shady, problematic. What's really problematic about them is their potential to undermine our project of enacting an intelligible and authentic self in joint improvisation with other self-enacters. But the exigencies of joint improvisation are complicated; the constraints on lawmaking are simpler, while yielding similar results. The Categorical Imperative clarifies the problem and points to an intelligible solution.

So understood, the rational force of the Imperative is not that which is attributed to it in Kantian theory. The Imperative is not an absolute or overriding requirement of rationality, like the laws of logic, which must never be violated. It is rather a desideratum in the practical reasoning of rational agents interacting with one another.

But perhaps the absolute force of the Imperative is also part of the idealization. The agents who act under an absolute requirement – the requirement to follow practical guidance that could be common knowledge – are the idealized agents, the frictionless surfaces and point-particles of the practical realm. We use the model of agents so constrained to help us understand what we are doing in the messy real world of joint improvisation. And in applying the model of agents absolutely constrained, we find ourselves constrained less than absolutely, somewhat as the real surfaces and particles of the physical world find themselves less than fully constrained by the laws of zero friction and zero extension.

Although the Categorical Imperative has overriding force only in the idealization, it is objective and a priori not just in the idealization but in reality as well. For it emanates from the exigencies of collective improvisation, which is the inescapable condition of agents interacting with other agents. Developing a shared basis for self-understanding is not a contingent aim that such agents can dispense with, even experimentally; rather, this aim is constitutive of their every experiment, in which they test some new way of understanding themselves, given the necessity of doing so together. Their need for a shared basis of self-understanding generates particular, structural reasons that are inescapable for agents – not just willed to be authoritative but found to be so, because they are embedded in their nature as social agents. These objective and a priori reasons are idealized by Kantian theory as issuing from the constraints on legislation in the Kingdom of Ends.

My interpretation of Kant suggests that if systematic theories of morality have a role to play, it is the role of idealizations clarifying how our methods of joint self-understanding introduce moral themes and patterns into our way of life. Can such a role be found for an alternative moral theory such as Utilitarianism? Maybe – though not with equal plausibility, in my view.

What Utilitarianism idealizes in our methods of self-understanding is the widespread use of desire-belief explanation, which supplies the consequentialist structure found in the Principle of Utility. Mammalian psychology being what it is, much of our behavior is best understood as directed at some outcome that we desire, via means that we believe conducive to attaining it. What we want, and how we believe it can be attained, will often be sufficient to determine what it makes sense to do, because we find ourselves in many situations that engage our desires but not our long-term plans or policies, customs, traits of character, emotions, or other potential springs of behavior. Doing what makes sense in these circumstances will consist in doing what, in our view, would maximize desire satisfaction. So if we follow a rule of maximizing desire satisfaction in these circumstances, in which belief-desire explanation is the predominant mode of self-understanding, we will approximate the outcome of even the most exhaustive practical reasoning.[14]

There are many contexts in which desire-belief explanation is overshadowed by other modes of self-understanding, since what it makes sense to do is not to pursue desired outcomes but rather to express feelings, to articulate convictions, to fall back on habits, to remain true to character, or simply to follow the way things are done hereabouts. Even so, the pressure toward unifying our self-understanding tends to make our convictions, habits, and traits at least consistent with our desires, so that doing what makes sense in the former terms amounts to acting as if to make sense in the latter as well. Actions that would be most accurately explained as manifesting habits or traits that have been coordinated with our desires can be explained to a rough approximation as maximizing desire-satisfaction itself.

Furthermore, what it makes sense to desire will often correspond to what it makes sense to be glad about, to celebrate, to boast of – in short, what it makes sense to approve of – and so it will tend to correspond to our application of words like 'good', used to express general approval. Since our desires and other attitudes of approval are regulated for intelligibility, we do not just call their objects good; we find them to be good, in the sense that I explained in Lecture 2. So we can attain a rough and approximate self-understanding if we conceive of ourselves as finding what's good and maximizing it.

Finally, the pressure toward sharing self-understandings with our partners in joint improvisation favors finding things that it

---

[14] For a more detailed version of this point, see my paper "The Story of Rational Action," *Philosophical Topics* 21 (1993): 229–53; reprinted in *The Possibility of Practical Reason* (Oxford: Oxford University Press, 2000), 170–99.

makes sense to desire and approve in common. We are consequently encouraged to converge wherever possible on a single
conception of what is good, and then to converge on pursuing it.

All of these pressures, if fully effective in our individual characters and shared way of life, would make us susceptible to a
consequentialist idealization, according to which we are jointly
finding things good and maximizing their realization. Myself, I
do not believe that we really are susceptible to this idealization,
because I do not believe that the pressures toward becoming
so are fully effective in our characters and way of life, or can
be fully effective given the constraints of human nature. Too
much of human life is governed by emotions, convictions, commitments, and practices that cannot be fully coordinated with
desire and that consequently elude idealization by consequentialism. I therefore believe that applying the consequentialist
idealization globally, and attempting to bear it out globally in
practice, inevitably leads to self-misunderstanding and inauthenticity. The consequentialist idealization is best reserved for
specific contexts in which desire-belief explanation is the order
of the day.

Consequentialists will respond that their principle is not
meant to represent all of our actual behavior. They propose an
alternative, "indirect" form of consequentialism, which I will
consider in a moment. First let me introduce the Utilitarian
brand of consequentialism, which is also usually defended in
indirect form.

Utilitarianism further strains the consequentialist idealization
by adding a specification of the good that we are idealized as
desiring and pursuing: the good is specified as the sum (or aver-
age) of benefits (minus costs) for everyone, weighted equally.
The question, from my perspective, is whether we have anything to gain in self-understanding by conceiving of ourselves

as maximizing the bottom line in a universal cost-benefit accounting.

I think not. Even if we can understand ourselves as acting to maximize – or, at least, as if to maximize – something jointly found to be good, what we jointly find to be good need not be the greatest sum of benefits for everyone. I haven't offered an account of harm and benefit in these lectures: my account of value did not include the personal-relative value of being good or bad *for* a person, hence beneficial or harmful.[15] But never mind the analysis of harm and benefit; what's at issue here is whether the greatest sum of benefits to everyone is what it makes sense for us jointly to desire and pursue. I simply doubt whether characters aiming to maximize the aggregate utility make much sense for us to enact as human beings.

Now, Utilitarians often say that their theory does not propose aggregate utility as an end-in-view, to be desired and pursued in practice.[16] The end of aggregate utility is to be promoted indirectly, by the pursuit of other ends, whose pursuit can be judged for its conduciveness to the aggregate utility, but only from a philosophical perspective that is occupied rarely, if ever, and perhaps not by everyone. Most of the time, we value the subordinate ends for their own sake, without regard to aggregate utility.

The problem with this claim, from my perspective, is that it requires an unreasonably realist conception of value. In my view, what is valuable is that which is rationally to-be-valued, in the sense that it makes sense to value it in some way. What it does not make sense for us to desire and pursue – or to admire, cherish, envy, celebrate, or whatever – is not to-be-valued and hence not valuable. Insofar as aggregate utility is pushed out of sight,

---

[15] Were I to offer such an account, it would say that what is good for a person is what it makes sense to want out of love for that person. See my "Beyond Price," *Ethics* 118 (2008): 191–212.

[16] See, e.g., Peter Railton, "Alienation, Consequentialism, and the Demands of Morality," *Philosophy and Public Affairs* 13 (1984): 134–71.

leaving other ends as the targets of our evaluative responses, it is
at risk of losing the role in practical reasoning that would constitute it as valuable.

＊　＊　＊

Well, maybe it makes sense for everyone to value aggregate utility some of the time. Maybe all of us retreat now and then to a
detached point of view, sheltered from the whirl of daily activity,
in which we expressly reflect on our way of life for the sake of
considering how to revise and update it. Maybe that reflective
enterprise would make most sense to us if guided by the end-in-
view of maximizing the sum of benefits to everyone.

Or maybe aggregate utility is valued, not by actual agents,
but by idealized agents, populating a Kingdom of Maximizers
analogous to the Kantian Kingdom of Ends. What use might we
have for such an idealization? Here is one possibility.

Each of us is likely to propose self-serving innovations in our
shared store of scenarios, and others will of course try to nudge
the repertoire in their own self-interested directions. Given our
need to converge on a repertoire, and the loss of intelligibility
that results from personal exemptions and exceptions, our jos-
tling for influence will have to end in compromise of some sort.
Maybe we can better understand this process by imagining that
the collective pressure of individual self-interest amounts to an
Invisible Hand guiding social change in the aggregate interest of all. Maybe imagining ourselves as agents of this Invisible
Hand would help us to understand what we're up to as we collaborate and compete to shape our shared way of life.

＊　＊　＊

I've done my best for Utilitarianism, but I must confess to
being unconvinced. Even in its indirect formulation, it does not
strike me as a useful idealization of the forces by which joint

self-improvisation gives moral shape to our individual characters or our shared way of life. And if Utilitarianism has no use as an idealization, then I don't know what use it has, since morality itself cannot be stated in a principle, being in fact a family of themes implicit in the ways of being and doing that we work out in joint improvisation.

Kant's Kingdom of Ends strikes me as a useful idealization of this process, because it requires shared bases for self-understanding, which are indeed required by our very nature as social agents. As players enacting ourselves together with other self-enacters, we cannot escape the need for a frame that contains common knowledge about who is doing what with whom. Hence we cannot escape the need to act in ways that are admissible into such a frame – which are, in effect, actions whose maxims can serve as legislation in a Kingdom of Ends.

7

Meaning

I have claimed that a rational agent resembles an improvisational actor in that he tries to make sense in causal-psychological terms, by acting in ways that can be understood as caused by his motives, habits, and other characteristics. But a theatrical improviser tries to be intelligible in an additional sense. For he tries to further the arc of the drama by doing things that will make for a good story, and they will make for a good story if they can be comprehended, or "grasped together," in the shape of a narrative. Does a rational agent resemble a theatrical actor in this respect as well, by aiming to make sense in narrative terms?

I assume that narrative intelligibility requires psychological intelligibility but not vice versa. That is, a story requires action, and action has to be intelligible as caused by the attitudes and attributes of a character, lest it count as no more than mere behavior, like blushing, sneezing, and fainting, which do not make for a story. Some theorists of narrative, following Aristotle, believe that causal intelligibility is all that's required for a story. If they are right, then making causal-psychological sense would already amount to making narrative sense as well. And in that case, the rational agent would already share the theatrical actor's concern for storytelling, simply by being concerned for making sense in causal-psychological terms. But I think that the Aristotelian theorists are mistaken: causal explanation and storytelling convey fundamentally different modes of understanding. Consequently, an agent can make sense in causal-psychological terms without making narrative sense (though as I've said, he can't make narrative sense without first making sense psychologically).

Yet when an agent tries to make narrative sense, that effort is inextricable from his practical reasoning, as I conceive it. He envisions a course of action that he would understand not just psychologically but as the next episode in his story, and then he enacts what he has envisioned, so that he understands what he is doing – understands it, again, not just in terms of his psychological attitudes and attributes but also as a continuation of the story.

This wrinkle in my conception of practical reasoning will be the topic of the present, final lecture. First I will explain why I believe that narrative understanding of action is distinct from causal-psychological understanding.[1] Then I will consider how the inclusion of narrative in an agent's self-understanding affects my conception of practical reasoning. Its effect is to fragment practical reasoning to some extent.

According to Aristotle, what makes a portrayal of events hang together as a story is a plot, or *muthos*, which requires the portrayed events to follow one another "by necessity or probability." The necessities and probabilities that Aristotle has in mind appear to be of the kind that could be revealed instead by a scientific explanation:[2]

> Plots are either simple or complex. ... The action, proceeding in the way defined, as one continuous whole, I call simple, when the change in the hero's fortunes takes place without Peripety

---

[1] The following discussion of narrative is excerpted from my "Narrative Explanation," *The Philosophical Review* 112 (2003): 1–25.

[2] Aristotle, *Poetics*, trans. Ingram Bywater, in *The Basic Works of Aristotle*, ed. Richard McKeon (New York: Random House, 1941), x, 1452a.

[Reversal] or Discovery; and complex, when it involves one or the other, or both. These should each of them arise out of the structure of the Plot itself, so as to be the consequence, necessary or probable, of the antecedents. There is a great difference between a thing happening *propter hoc* and *post hoc*.

If Aristotle is right, then a plot must convey understanding in the same way that it qualifies as a plot to begin with – namely, by providing each event with antecedents from which to follow as a necessary or probable consequence. And the understanding conveyed by a plot, in that case, would be no different from that conveyed by other genres of explanation.

This view is implicit in famous remarks by E. M. Forster on the plotting of a novel:[3]

"The king died and then the queen died," is a story. "The king died and then the queen died of grief" is a plot. ... Consider the death of the queen. If it is in a story we say "and then?" If it is in a plot we ask "why?" That is the fundamental difference between these two aspects of the novel.

An answer to the question "why?" is of course an explanation. Hence Forster conceives of a plot as a form of explanation, and he seems to have causal explanation in mind, since the element that makes for a plot, in his example, is the queen's grief, which is a causal link between her death and the king's.

This view of narrative has been elaborated by Noël Carroll, in a paper entitled "On the Narrative Connection."[4] Following Morton White, Carroll distinguishes among three modes of discourse for recounting events: *annals*, which represent events as temporally ordered; *chronicles*, which represent temporally

3 *Aspects of the Novel* (New York: Harcourt Brace and Company, 1927), 130. As I shall explain below, I have been using the term 'story' as extensionally equivalent to Forster's term 'plot'. What Forster here calls a "story," I would prefer to call a "tale."
4 In *Beyond Aesthetics: Philosophical Essays* (Cambridge: Cambridge University Press, 2001), 118–33.

ordered events pertaining to a single subject; and *narrative*, which requires some additional connection among the events:

> If I say, "I woke up; later I dressed; still later I went to class," I suspect that most people would agree that this falls short of a full-fledged narrative, although the events cited might be turned into ingredients of a narrative. But why isn't it a narrative properly so called? To put it vaguely – because the connection among the events alluded to by it is not tight enough. (pp. 119–20)

The connection that is "tight enough" to transform a chronicle into a narrative, according to Carroll, is the connection between causes and the effects for which they were, in the circumstances, necessary (though perhaps not sufficient). Carroll illustrates the need for such "narrative connections" by means of the following example:

> Consider this putative narrative: "Aristarchus hypothesized the heliocentric theory thereby anticipating Copernicus' discovery by many centuries." ... If there is no line of influence stretching from Aristarchus' discovery to Copernicus', I, at least, find it strained to think that this is narrative. It is an interesting series of events. Indeed, mention of the second event in this series retrospectively reveals something of the significance of the earlier event, and ... retrospective significance is a frequently occurring feature of narrative. However, where the events bear no sort of causal relation to each other, they seem more of the order of coincidence than of narrative. ... (p. 125)

> [R]etrospective significance, though a typically recurring and explicable feature of narrative, should not be mistaken as the mark of narrative. For the temporally ordered discourse "Aristarchus hypothesized the heliocentric system and then centuries later Copernicus discovered it again" affords the apprehension of retrospective significance – it indicates the point of mentioning Aristarchus' discovery in light of Copernicus' – but it is not, as I have argued, a narrative proper inasmuch as it lacks a narrative connection. (p. 127)

In Carroll's terminology, the discoveries of Aristarchus and Copernicus are ingredients for a chronicle but not for a narrative, because they are successive events pertaining to a common topic but are causally unrelated. Carroll thinks that the successive events in a narrative must occur not just *post hoc* but also *propter hoc*. Carroll goes on to suggest that the causal content of a narrative underlies its explanatory potential:[5]

> Perhaps a related consideration in favor of my view of narrative is that narrative is a common form of explanation. In ordinary speech, we use narratives to explain how things happened and why certain standing conditions were important. Narrative is capable of performing this role because it tracks causal networks. ... Thus, insofar as what we call narratives are explanatory, it seems advisable to regard narrative properly so called as connected to causation and not merely temporal succession. (p. 128)

Here Carroll states the view that I have called mistaken, that the explanatory force of a narrative is due to information that would be equally explanatory if recast as a causal explanation. I believe that there is explanatory force peculiar to the narrative form itself.

My skepticism about Carroll's conception of the narrative connection is aroused, to begin with, by his example of a nonstory. I agree with Carroll that he doesn't really tell a story when he says, "Aristarchus hypothesized the heliocentric theory thereby anticipating Copernicus' discovery by many centuries." Yet this sentence may fall short of being a story, not because it describes events that are causally unrelated, but because it merely alludes to the second event by way of characterizing the first, without ever asserting that the second occurred. Even the shortest story must recount more than one event.

5 See also Carl G. Hempel, "The Function of General Laws in History," in *Aspects of Scientific Explanation and Other Essays in the Philosophy of Science* (New York: The Free Press, 1965), 231–43.

This account of Carroll's failure to tell a story does not apply to his second attempt, which goes like this: "Aristarchus hypothesized the heliocentric system and then centuries later Copernicus discovered it again." Here Carroll recounts two events, one after the other, and yet he claims that he still hasn't told a story. I don't know whether to accept this claim, but it is in any case considerably weaker than what Carroll is committed to claiming. He is committed to claiming, not just that he hasn't told a story about Aristarchus and Copernicus, but that there is no true story to be told about them, given their mutual isolation in the web of causality. I am not convinced: I am fairly certain that one could tell a story about these events, and without inventing a causal connection that wasn't there.

Consider Aristotle's example of a disjointed story:

> Tragedy, however, is an imitation not only of a complete action, but also of incidents arousing pity and fear. Such incidents have the very greatest effect on the mind when they occur unexpectedly and at the same time in consequence of one another; there is more of the marvelous in them then than if they happened of themselves or by mere chance. Even matters of chance seem most marvelous if there is an appearance of design as it were in them; as for instance the statue of Mitys at Argos killed the author of Mitys' death by falling down on him when a looker-on at a public spectacle; for incidents like that we think to be not without a meaning. [*Poetics* ix, 1452a]

Here Aristotle is trying to reconcile the requirement that plotted events follow "by necessity or probability," on the one hand, with the requirement that they arouse fear and pity, on the other, given that these emotions are enhanced by the element of surprise. The usual way to reconcile these requirements, according to Aristotle, is to have the plotted events "occur unexpectedly and at the same time in consequence of one another." Another way of obtaining the same effect, however, is for causally unrelated events to have what Aristotle calls "an appearance of design," as when a murderer is accidentally killed by a statue of his victim.

Surely, the death of Mitys' murderer makes for a good story. We might interpret Aristotle as claiming that the "appearance of design" in this story is actually an appearance of causality or probability, because the audience is led to imagine an avenging spirit, or some other force of cosmic justice, behind the falling statue. But I think that the story holds up even under an absurdist reading, which takes the murderer's death for an accident. On this reading, the murder of Mitys and the death of his murderer are no more connected than the discoveries of Aristarchus and Copernicus. Even so, the one pair of disjointed events seems like more of a story than the other. Something is present in Aristotle's pair of events that's missing from Carroll's, and it needn't be an imagined causal connection. What is it?

The crucial difference between these examples, I think, is that in Aristotle's the sequence of events completes an emotional cadence in the audience. When a murder is followed by a fitting comeuppance, we feel indignation gratified. Although these events follow no causal sequence, they provide an emotional resolution, and so they have a meaning for the audience, despite lacking any causal or probabilistic connection. No similar emotional cadence is resolved by Copernicus' rediscovery of what Aristarchus had previously discovered – not, at least, in Carroll's telling. The possibility in principle of fashioning these discoveries into a story is due to the possibility of finding something that they might mean to an audience in emotional terms.

Any sequence of events, no matter how improbable, can provide material for storytelling if it completes an emotional cadence. Twins separated at birth are ideal protagonists for a story even if their eventual reunion is a fluke. A discovery due to serendipity, a tragedy narrowly averted by dumb luck, a mundane act that unforeseeably becomes the last in a life accidentally cut short – these are the stuff not only of literary storytelling but of

legend, gossip, and other forms of everyday narrative. Whether
a winning lottery ticket or a fatal house fire makes enough of a
story to be featured on the local news depends, not on whether
its causes can be told, but rather on whether the surrounding
circumstances will call up feelings that can be brought to some
resolution by this inexplicable stroke of good or bad fortune. So
long as we feel an anxiety relieved or a hope dashed, we have the
sense of hearing a story, even if we have no idea of why events
took the relevant turn. Similarly in Forster's example, the king's
death need not have contributed to the queen's in order to provide material for a story. Let the queen laugh at the king's death
and later slip on a fatal banana peel: the audience will experience the resolution characteristic of a plot.

It is no coincidence, I think, that in transforming Forster's nonstory into a story, I have made it sound like a joke. Joke telling is one
genre of storytelling. Attempts to generalize about the internal
logic of jokes are notoriously ill-conceived: there is no particular
way that a stretch of discourse or its subject matter must be con-
structed in order for it to qualify as a joke. What makes a stretch
of discourse into a joke is that it reliably brings the audience to
the resolution of laughter, by means of whatever internal logic or
illogic it can. In my view, a stretch of discourse can qualify as a
story, more generally, by reliably producing in the audience some
emotional resolution, of which laughter is just one example.

The emotional resolution that is essential to the story form
occurs, of course, at the end. The idea that stories are structured by their endings has long been familiar among literary
critics. Frank Kermode gives a vivid illustration of the idea in his
lectures entitled *The Sense of an Ending*.[6]

---

[6] *The Sense of an Ending: Studies in the Theory of Fiction* (New York: Oxford
University Press, 2000), 4–45.

Let us take a very simple example, the ticking of a clock. We ask what it *says:* and we agree that it says *tick-tock.* By this fiction we humanize it, make it talk our language. Of course, it is we who provide the fictional difference between the two sounds; *tick* is our word for a physical beginning, *tock* our word for an end. ... It can be shown by experiment that subjects who listen to rhythmic structures such as *tick-tock*, repeated identically, 'can reproduce the intervals within the structure accurately, but they cannot grasp spontaneously the interval between the rhythmic groups,' that is, between *tock* and *tick*, even when this remains constant.[7] The first interval is organized and limited, the second not. ... The fact that we call the second of the two related sounds *tock* is evidence that we use fictions to enable the end to confer organization and form on the temporal structure. The interval between the two sounds is now charged with significant duration. The clock's *tick-tock* I take to be a model of what we call a plot, an organization that humanizes time by giving it form; and the interval between *tock* and *tick* represents purely successive, disorganized time of the sort that we need to humanize.

Kermode's example is highly suggestive but doesn't really explain what makes for an ending. Why is *tock* the ending and *tick* the beginning, rather than vice versa, or neither?

A critic who has attempted to answer this question is Peter Brooks, who likens the cadence of a narrative to the vicissitudes of an instinct in Freudian theory.[8] The beginning of a story, according to Brooks, is like the stimulus that prompts the search for stimulus reduction, the itch that demands scratching; the middle is like the postponement of stimulus reduction by obstacles and misdirected efforts; and the end is like the satisfying discharge that pacifies, if only temporarily. I think that Brooks is right to look for the nature of endings in the nature of human affect, but I also think that his focus on Freud's theory of

---

7 Here Kermode is quoting Paul Fraisse, *The Psychology of Time* (New York: Harper and Row, 1964).

8 *Reading for the Plot* (New York: Knopf, 1984), Chapter 4, "Freud's Masterplot: A Model for Narrative."

instinct is unduly narrow and controversial. Freudian theory is not needed to support the simple observation that human affect follows a cycle of provocation, complication, and resolution.

Ronald de Sousa has proposed what might seem like the inverse of Brooks's analysis: whereas Brooks analyzes narrative in terms of affect, de Sousa analyzes affect in terms of narrative, hypothesizing that each human emotion has a "paradigm scenario":[9]

> We are made familiar with the vocabulary of emotion by association with *paradigm scenarios.* These are drawn first from our daily life as small children and later reinforced by the stories, art, and culture to which we are exposed. Later still, in literate cultures, they are supplemented and refined by literature. Paradigm scenarios involve two aspects: first, a situation type ..., and second, a set of characteristic or "normal" *responses* to the situation, where normality is first a biological matter and then very quickly becomes a cultural one.

De Sousa envisions that these scenarios are stored in memory and retrieved as a means of understanding what we experience: they are "not so much stories up for interpretation as stories *in terms of which* other stories and situations are themselves interpreted."[10] When brought to bear on a situation, paradigm scenarios determine what we focus on, what we tend to notice, and how we are disposed to respond: "When a paradigm scenario suggests itself as an interpretation of a current situation, it arranges or rearranges our perceptual, cognitive, and inferential dispositions."[11]

I want to borrow from Brooks and de Sousa, first, the idea that the earliest stories in our lives are about the vicissitudes of our emotions; and second, that the shape of those stories is determined, in the first instance, by the nature of human affect,

---

[9] *The Rationality of Emotion* (Cambridge, MA: MIT Press, 1987), 182. See also "Emotions, Education and Time," *Metaphilosophy* 21 (1990): 434–46. De Sousa refers to Schank's collaborator Robert Abelson at pp. 72–3 of *The Rationality of Emotion.*

[10] "Emotions, Education and Time," 438.

[11] *The Rationality of Emotion*, 201.

although it may subsequently be modified by cultural influences. The cadence that makes for a story is that of the arousal and resolution of affect, a pattern that is biologically programmed. Hence we understand stories viscerally, with our bodies.

The notion of visceral understanding is illustrated by Kermode's case of a ticking clock.[12] For I suggest that we understand the cadence of *tick-tock* with the muscles of our face and mouth, which are tensed for the first syllable and relaxed for the second.[13] The cycle of tension and relaxation is built in to the very nature of muscle, and it's what leads us to perceive *tick* as the beginning and *tock* as the end. In much the same way, we understand the cadence of a story with the natural cycles of our emotional sensibility.

* * *

An emotional cadence is something that unfolds over time. In this respect, it reflects the nature of emotion, which is

[12] See also Andrew Mead's "Bodily Hearing: Physiological Metaphors and Musical Understanding," *Journal of Music Theory* 43 (1999): 1–18, together with Kendall L. Walton, "Style and the Products and Processes of Art," in *The Concept of Style*, ed. Beryl Lang (Ithaca, NY: Cornell University Press, 1987), 72–103. Mead explains the metaphor of "high" and "low" pitches in terms of the muscular effort involved in their production.

[13] Many oscillating processes have onomatopoetic names with the same feature: "ding-dong," "sing-song," "flip-flop," "clip-clop," "ping-pong," "splish-splash," "pitter-patter," "zig-zag," "chit chat," "clickety-clack," "see-saw," "teeter-totter." Steven Pinker discusses this phenomenon in *The Language Instinct* (New York: William Morrow, 1994), pp. 166–9. (Thanks to John Steele for this reference.) Shelley Velleman has provided the following examples from other languages: "caceec-cacaac" (Khmer: to chatter, twitter); "toteh-totah" (Khmer: to toddle); "rojiing rojoong" and "roneeng ronoong" (Khmer: to sway, dangle); "bolak-bolik" (Indonesian: to and fro); "nplij-nploj" (Hmong: the popping sound of chewing gum); "kippadi-koppadi" (Estonian: clip-clop); "kill-koll" (Estonian: ding-dong); "killadi-kolladi" (Estonian: things clanging together); "killaki-kollaki" (Estonian: hammering sound); "kribu-krabu" (Estonian: scribbling); "ligadi-logadi" (Estonian: rickety).

essentially temporal. An emotion itself is something that unfolds over time. Each emotion unfolds differently, but some generalizations can be made about how emotions unfold.[14]

The first episode in the natural history of an emotion is its arousal by characteristic conditions. In this respect, emotions differ from some other motivational attitudes, such as desires. It is not in the nature of most desires to be elicited by conditions of any particular kind. From the fact that someone wants something, we cannot ordinarily infer how he came to want it; whereas from the fact that he is afraid, we can draw some plausible inferences about how he came to be in that state. The second episode in the history of an emotion is often a sequence of physiological symptoms, such as perspiration or accelerated heartbeat, often accompanied by distinctive feelings as well – a lump in the throat, a knot in the stomach, a tingling at the base of the spine. Then there are purely reflexive behavioral symptoms, including facial expressions, such as smiling or scowling; bodily postures, such as cringing; and various programmed behaviors, such as laughing, crying, or gagging. Equally reflexive are the associated patterns of attention and interpretation of the sort mentioned by de Sousa: a heightened awareness of danger, for example, or greater sensitivity to physical beauty. Next come motivational dispositions toward behaviors that can be performed in the form of deliberate actions, though they may also issue impulsively under the force of an overwhelming urge: gamboling, fleeing, attacking, caressing, and so on. Finally, each emotion has a characteristic pattern of decay and extinction, involving conditions that characteristically dispel it, and the mental states that characteristically remain in its wake.

[14] Here I am drawing on the "affect program" theory of emotion. See Craig DeLancy, *Passionate Engines: What Emotions Reveal about Mind and Artificial Intelligence* (Oxford: Oxford University Press, 2002).

The diachronic nature of emotion figures prominently in Aristotle's *Poetics* – specifically, in his requirement that the drama must elicit fear and pity and then bring them to an appropriate *katharsis* (vi 1449b). Yet Aristotle draws no explicit connection between the emotional vicissitudes of a tragedy and the structure of its *muthos*, or plot, which Aristotle analyzes into the elements of beginning, middle, and end. Brooks's thesis, which I am seeking to generalize, is that the diachronic nature of emotion underlies Aristotle's analysis of plot, because beginning, middle, and end must ultimately be defined in terms of the arousal and resolution of emotion.

This process needn't be confined to the arousal and resolution of a single emotion. One emotion often gives way to another: puzzlement to curiosity, curiosity to foreboding, foreboding to horror, horror to grief – or perhaps instead to anger, which gives way to resentment, and so on. Unlike a chain of causation, however, a sequence of emotions has beginnings and endings, because emotions naturally sort themselves into *ticks* and *tocks*. Emotions naturally qualify as initiatory or conclusory in virtue of various features, of which I will mention only a few.

Some emotions are aroused by circumstances independently of the subject's prior emotional state, whereas others register the impact of events on a prior emotion. Fear and anger, for example, can be elicited out of the blue, by danger and injury, respectively; whereas disappointment, gratification, and grief must develop out of some antecedent attitude that can be disappointed, gratified, or aggrieved. The intentional contents of the latter emotions often include their emotional antecedents. Disappointment conceives of its object as *having been hoped for*, grief conceives of its object as *having been loved*, and so on; whereas hope, fear, and anger need not conceive of their objects in terms of any prior affect.

Emotions like hope, fear, and anger are by nature unstable, because they motivate behavior, or are elicited by circumstances, that ultimately lead to their extinction. Thus, fear motivates flight, which leads to the alleviation of fear; and hope is aroused by future prospects, which either materialize or not, turning hope into gratification or disappointment. By contrast, grief and gratification are stable, because their eliciting conditions and resulting behaviors are not conducive to change. Grief is a response to permanent loss, gratification a response to decisive gain, and neither emotion motivates efforts to alter its causes. Hence grief and gratification, although they tend to fade with time, neither lead to nor result from a process that replaces them with other emotions.

These differences among emotions allow for some broad generalizations. Fear can initiate or continue an emotional sequence, but it cannot resolve one; grief can resolve an emotional sequence, but it rarely initiates one. The reason is that fear can be aroused out of the blue and then motivates behavior that leads to further emotional developments; whereas grief develops out of prior attitudes, and alludes to them, but tends not to be an engine of emotional change.

Suppose, then, that the emotion of pity, as it figures in Aristotle's account of tragedy, is the audience's compassionate response to a character's grief. In that case, Aristotle's requirement that a tragedy arouse fear and pity would amount to the requirement that it lead its audience from an essentially initiatory emotion to an essentially conclusory one – from an emotional *tick* to an emotional *tock*. The emotions of fear and pity, in Aristotle's account of tragedic emotion, would therefore correspond to the beginning and ending in his account of tragedic plot.

*   *   *

I have now put forward two premises of an inference. The first premise is that the understanding provided by narrative is attributable to the nature of narrative itself – to that in virtue of which a recounting of events qualifies as a story. The second premise is that a description of events qualifies as a story in virtue of its power to initiate and resolve an emotional sequence in the audience. What follows from these premises is that the power to initiate and resolve an emotional sequence ought to endow narrative with its power to render events intelligible. But how?

To begin with, the sequence of emotions through which a story leads its audience is typically a familiar sequence, such as the sequence that I outlined earlier, from puzzlement to curiosity to foreboding to dismay to grief (a sequence that underlies, for example, the plot of *Oedipus Rex).*[15] A story therefore enables its audience to assimilate events, not to familiar patterns of *how things happen*, but rather to familiar patterns of *how*

---

[15] Here I am disagreeing with those who regard stories as providing our initial acquaintance with emotions and emotional processes. For example, Martha Nussbaum writes:

[S]ince we are all tellers of stories, and since one of the child's most pervasive and powerful ways of learning its society's values and structures is through the stories it hears and learns to tell, stories will be a major source of any culture's emotional life. What fear or love *is* will be, for a child … a construct out of stories, the intersection, the somewhat confused amalgam of those stories. Stories first construct and then evoke (and strengthen) the experience of feeling. ("Narrative Emotions: Beckett's Genealogy of Love," *Ethics* 98 [1988]: 225–54, pp. 233–4)

[I]f stories are … primary vehicles of emotion teaching, then we might say that to have an emotion will be (or centrally involve) the acceptance of a certain sort of story. (p. 235)

I do not agree that stories construct what fear or love is for a child. Fear, certainly, and possibly also love are basic emotions whose nature is largely determined antecedently to acculturation. I do believe that basic emotions are subject to cultural elaboration, which may be accomplished by stories, among other means. Although anger is a pre-cultural endowment of all human beings, road rage is not; although jealousy may be a basic emotion, it's unclear whether envy is, and it's likely that *Schadenfreude* is not. No doubt, someone could learn *Schadenfreude* from stories, but I see no reason to suppose that storytelling is essential to learning it.

things feel. These patterns are not themselves stored in discursive form, as scenarios or stories: they are stored rather in experiential, proprioceptive, and kinesthetic memory—as we might say, in the muscle memory of the heart.[16] Although the audience may have no discursive memory of events such as those of the story, it nevertheless has an experience of *déja senti,* because its emotional sensibility naturally follows the ups and downs of the story, just as a muscle naturally follows the cycle of tension and release.

What's more, the emotion that resolves a narrative sequence tends to subsume the emotions that preceded it: the triumph felt at a happy ending is the triumph of ambitions realized and anxieties allayed; the grief felt at a tragic ending is the grief of hopes dashed or loves denied. Hence the conclusory emotion in a narrative sequence embodies not just how the audience feels about the ending; it embodies how the audience feels, at the ending, about the whole story. Having passed through the emotional ups and downs of the story, as one event succeeded another, the audience comes to rest in a stable attitude about the series of events in its entirety.

Thus, the audience of a story understands the narrated events, first, because it *knows how they feel,* in the sense that it experiences them as leading it through a natural emotional sequence; and second, because it *knows how it feels about them,* in the sense that it arrives at a stable attitude toward them overall. The audience may or may not understand how the narrated events came about, but it understands what they mean – what they mean, that is, to the audience itself, in emotional terms.

This conception of narrative has a significant upshot for my view of practical reasoning, since it implies that practical reasoning

---

[16] Here I make a decisive departure from de Sousa.

is fragmented into the pursuit of two asymmetrically dependent modes of self-understanding. I think that we aim to make sense of ourselves not just in the mode of causal explanation but also in the mode of storytelling.[17] We consequently aim to do things for which we have both an explanation, revealing why we came to do them, and a narrative that helps to clarify how we feel about them or what they mean to us.

The most common way in which we seek meaning in our actions is by seeking to make our future continuous with our past, even at the expense of instrumental rationality. We repeatedly commit what economists call the fallacy of sunk costs – in vernacular terms, throwing good money after bad.[18]

From the perspective of instrumental rationality, in which we understand our actions in terms of their motivating aims, throwing good money after bad is indeed irrational, since it foreseeably tends to frustrate our aims and therefore cannot be understood as motivated by them. Having already invested attention and effort in an unpromising endeavor lends no intelligibility to the course of investing more, given motives that are focused on future payoffs.

If we sought to understand our decisions only in instrumental terms, we would have no reason to seek a future that continues the narrative arc of our past. We would be rationally obliged to invest each successive ounce of attention or effort in whichever endeavors offered the greatest expected future returns, irrespective of where we had invested before. Spending another day in a marriage or degree program or career would be irrational if it could be spent more profitably elsewhere.

---

[17] For further discussion of the ideas presented below, see my "Well-Being and Time," *The Pacific Philosophical Quarterly* 72 (1991): 48–77; reprinted in *The Possibility of Practical Reason* (Oxford: Oxford University Press, 2000), 56–84.

[18] For a similar view of the so-called sunk cost fallacy, see Elizabeth Anderson, *Value in Ethics and Economics* (Cambridge, MA: Harvard University Press, 1993), 35.

One counterweight to opportunism of this sort is the rational inertia of commitments, which I discussed in Lecture 4. Abandoning projects and relationships as soon as their prospects dimmed would undermine our grounds for expecting to follow through on future projects and relationships, thereby undermining our ability to understand making investments in projects or relationships at all. I think that narrative practical reasoning provides a further counterweight to opportunism. We stick with a marriage or a degree program after it has stopped promising to repay our efforts partly because even the story of eventual failure provides the emotional cadence of hopes disappointed, which has a comprehensible meaning. As any A.B.D. student knows, an endeavor abandoned in midcourse yields no emotional resolution. Continually abandoning one relationship or project for another would leave us not knowing (as we might say) what some parts of our lives had been about. And to know what parts of our lives have been "about" is just to know how they fit into a story with an emotionally intelligible arc.

Another common case of narrative rationality is learning from misfortune. People say, "If life hands you a lemon, make lemonade." That sounds like the fallacy of sunk costs again. If life hands you a lemon, the instrumentally rational course may be to throw it away and look for a kumquat instead. Why feel obliged to make something out of a lemon just because you've been handed one? The answer is that a misfortune can be given meaning by a narrative that incorporates it into the remainder of your life, during which its bitterness is still detectable but somehow sweetened. Accidents and illnesses are bad things, but they don't have to be surd interruptions to life, leaving an unresolved emotional residue of frustration. You can retrospectively give them a completed emotional meaning by making them the source of something that you want to carry with you going forward.

These distinct modes of practical reasoning make us susceptible to distinct modes of bad faith. One mode is that of Sartre's waiter, whom I discussed in Lecture 1. He chains his actions together as if they are determined by a mechanism within him rather than by his idea of how a waiter would act – and hence as if they weren't his idea. The other mode is that of the self-dramatizing agent who pretends that his tale of woe is a story in which he finds himself rather than casts himself, his fate rather than his composition.[19] In the former case, the self-deceived agent grasps at a false psychological self-understanding; in the latter, he sacrifices psychological self-understanding for the sake of his narrative. The latter case thus illustrates the importance of harmonizing these modes of self-understanding: insofar as the story one lives out is of one's own composition, one had better live out a story that one can explain having chosen to compose.

Narrative self-understanding is not a substitute for causal-psychological self-understanding. The tale of Oedipus makes for a good story even if we don't understand why the prophecy of Tiresias came true; but the tale would make no sense of any kind if we didn't understand, from one scene to the next, why Oedipus was behaving as he did – leaving Corinth, killing a stranger, marrying a queen, and so forth. And although Mitys' comeuppance had no causal explanation under that description, it didn't consist in an inexplicable piece of behavior on his part. Events can be both narratively intelligible and causally inscrutable, in other words, but not in the very same respects. In particular, we are unlikely to find emotional meaning in behavior to which we cannot give a psychological interpretation.

Hence practical reasoning aimed at narrative self-understanding can supplement but not replace reasoning aimed at self-understanding in causal-psychological terms. And I

[19] On the dangers of narrative self-understanding, see Hannah Arendt, "Isak Denisen," in *Men in Dark Times* (New York: Harcourt Brace and Co., 1983), 95–109.

suspect that this supplementary mode of practical reasoning is optional, at least to some extent. Some people prefer lives that are uniformly desirable and narratively flat, like the weather in southern California; others prefer lives that are like the weather in New England, where the story of death and rebirth is retold on a regular basis. I see no reason why rationality shouldn't come in many different complexions, with varying proportions of the forms that self-understanding can take.[20]

Here I have accepted a mild version of David Enoch's "shmagency" thesis without, I think, weakening my conception of agency. As I explained in Lecture 5, Enoch objects to the Kantian strategy of ending the regress of practical justification in an aim that is constitutive of agency, on the grounds that agency itself would need to be justified in contrast to some alternative constitution, which Enoch dubs "shmagency."[21] I don't think that this objection requires an answer until it specifies an alternative that is remotely plausible as a constitution that we could in fact instantiate and that would endow us with something like agency. If such an alternative is specified, my answer to the objection will be that it requires us to make a choice or a *shmoice*, depending on which constitution we currently instantiate, and that our choice or *shmoice* will have to be guided by the aim constitutive of which one it is. Arriving at one or the other constitution in a manner constituted by no aim, and hence subject to no criterion of success, would be merely to pick a constitution rather than to make a choice or a *shmoice*; and picking never calls for a justification, because it cannot be correct or incorrect. What is not possible is to resolve the question in a manner that can be correct or incorrect, and that consequently calls for justification, but not in relation to a criterion inherent in the kind of resolution it is.

[20] See Galen Strawson, "Against Narrativity," *Ratio* 17 (2004): 428–52.
[21] "Agency, Shmagency: Why Normativity Won't Come from What Is Constitutive of Action," *Philosophical Review* 115 (2) (2006): 169–98.

The possibility of narrative self-understanding, and hence narrative practical reasoning, illustrates this point. If we are exclusively causal-psychological self-interpreters, we can still ask ourselves whether we wouldn't make more sense, psychologically speaking, if we took a greater interest in narrative sources of meaning in our lives. If, alternatively, we seek not only to explain ourselves but also to narrate our lives, we might ask ourselves whether the mix between modes of self-understanding that we currently seek wouldn't be best achieved by seeking a different mix – whether, for example, the most narratable life of the most explicable protagonist wouldn't be one in which he chose at this point to care somewhat less about narrativity.

Why would I give up on completing this particular story? What would it mean, in the story, to have given up on it just now? And what would explain my focusing more on being explicable? Alternatively: Would compromising on explicability for the sake of the story be sufficiently explicable, given that I cannot entirely forgo explanation? Might it actually prevent the story from describing a meaningful arc?

I think that we ask ourselves such questions – though not of course in these terms – whenever we face the possibility of ruptures or radical discontinuities in our lives. We ask ourselves, What is the point of going on? What would be the point of making a break? And "the point" can be either the meaning or the motive – or a meaningful or a motivated combination of the two. I am not committed to there being uniquely correct answers to these questions. Practical reasoning is not an effective procedure for answering questions.

The ideal, of course, is to get the various forms of self-understanding to harmonize – to want what it makes sense for us to want; to pursue what we want, that being what it makes sense to pursue; to have other values that cohere with our wants and pursuits; to make those pursuits hang together as stories, so that we know how we feel about them in the end; and, finally, to manage all of this in the company of others who are trying to manage likewise, whom we must understand, and to whom we must make ourselves understood, if our interactions with them are to be intelligible. *That* is how we get along, in life and with one another.

Bibliography

Abelson, R. P., and Schank, R. C. *Scripts, Plans, Goals, and Understanding: An Inquiry into Human Knowledge Structures.* Hillsday, NJ: Lawrence Erlbaum Associates, 1977.

Adams, Robert Merrihew. *Finite and Infinite Goods.* Oxford: Oxford University Press, 1999.

Anderson, Elizabeth. *Value in Ethics and Economics.* Cambridge, MA: Harvard University Press, 1993.

Anscombe, G. E. M. *Intention.* Cambridge, MA: Harvard University Press, 2000.

Arendt, Hannah. "Isak Denisen." In *Men in Dark Times* (New York: Harcourt Brace and Co., 1983), 95–109.

Aristotle. *Poetics*, trans. Ingram Bywater. In *The Basic Works of Aristotle*, ed. Richard McKeon (New York: Random House, 1941), 1453–87.

Bicchieri, Christina. *The Grammar of Society: The Nature and Dynamics of Social Norms.* New York: Cambridge University Press, 2006.

Blackburn, Simon. *Ruling Passions.* Oxford: Clarendon Press, 1998.

Block, Gay, & Drucker, Malka. *Rescuers: Portraits of Moral Courage in the Holocaust.* New York: Holmes & Meier, 1992.

Boghossian, Paul. "How Are Objective Epistemic Reasons Possible?" *Philosophical Studies* **106** (2001): 340–80.

"Blind Reasoning." *Proceedings of the Aristotelian Society*, Supplementary Volume **77** (2003): 225–48.

Brodt, S. E., & Zimbardo, P. G. "Modifying Shyness-related Social Behavior through Symptom Misattribution." *Journal of Personality and Social Psychology* **41** (1981): 437–49.

Brooks, Peter. "Freud's Masterplot: A Model for Narrative." In *Reading for the Plot* (New York: Knopf, 1984), 90–112.

Cantor, J. R., Zillman, D., & Bryant, J. "Enhancement of Experienced Sexual Arousal in Response to Erotic Stimuli through Misattribution of Unrelated Residual Excitation.", *Journal of Personality and Social Psychology* **32** (1975): 69–75.

Carroll, Noël. "On the Narrative Connection." In *Beyond Aesthetics: Philosophical Essays* (Cambridge: Cambridge University Press, 2001), 118–33.

Castañeda, Hector-Neri. "Practical Thinking, Reasons for Doing, and Intentional Action: The Thinking of Doing and the Doing of Thinking." *Philosophical Perspectives* **4** (1990): 273–308.

Cavell, Stanley. "The Avoidance of Love: A Reading of King Lear." In *Must We Mean What We Say? A Book of Essays* (Cambridge: Cambridge University Press, 1976), 267–353.

Dancy, Jonathan. *Ethics without Principles.* Oxford: Clarendon Press, 2004.

D'Arms, Justin, & Jacobson, Daniel. "The Moralistic Fallacy: On the 'Appropriateness' of Emotions." *Philosophy and Phenomenological Research* **61** (2000): 65–90.

Darwall, Stephen L. "Autonomist Internalism and the Justication of Morals." *Nous* **24** (1990): 257–67.

Davidson, Donald. "Actions, Reasons and Causes." In *Essays on Actions and Events* (New York: Oxford University Press, 2001), 3–20.

DeLancy, Craig. *Passionate Engines: What Emotions Reveal about Mind and Artificial Intelligence.* Oxford: Oxford University Press, 2002.

Dennett, Daniel. "The Reality of Selves." In *Consciousness Explained* (Boston: Little, Brown and Company, 1991), 412–30.

de Sousa, Ronald. "Emotions, Education, and Time." *Metaphilosophy* **21** (1990): 434–46.

The Rationality of Emotion. Cambridge, MA: MIT Press, 1987.

Dreier, James. "Humean Doubts about the Practical Justification of Morality." In *Ethics and Practical Reason*, ed. Garrett Cullity and Berys Gaut (Oxford: Clarendon Press, 1997), 81–99.

Duclos, S. E., Laird, J. D., Schneider, E., Sexter, M., Stern, L., & Van Lighten, O. "Emotion-specific Effects of Facial Expressions and Postures on Emotional Experience." *Journal of Personality and Social Psychology* **57** (1989): 100–8.

Enoch, David. "Agency, Shmagency: Why Normativity Won't Come from What Is Constitutive of Action." *Philosophical Review* **115** (2006): 169–98.

Evans, Matthew. "The Lessons of Euthyphro 10a-11b" (MS).

Ferrero, Luca. "Constitutivism and the Inescapability of Agency." In *Oxford Studies in Metaethics*, Vol. 4, ed. Russ Shafer-Landau (New York: Oxford University Press, Forthcoming).

Forster, E. M. *Aspects of the Novel*. New York: Harcourt Brace and Company, 1927.

Fraisse, Paul. *The Psychology of Time*. London: Eyre and Spottiswoode, 1964.

Frankfurt, Harry. "The Problem of Action." *American Philosophical Quarterly* 15 (1978): 157–62; reprinted in *The Importance of What We Care About* (Cambridge: Cambrige University Press, 1988), 69–79.

"Rationality and the Unthinkable." In *The Importance of What We Care About* (Cambridge: Cambridge University Press, 1988), 177–90.

Freud, Sigmund. *Civilization and Its Discontents*. In *The Standard Edition of the Complete Psychological Works of Sigmund Freud* [S.E.], ed. James Strachey et al. (London: The Hogarth Press), Vol. 21: 59–145.

Group Psychology and the Analysis of the Ego, S.E. Vol. 18: 65–143.

New Introductory Lectures, S.E. Vol. 22.

An Outline of Psychoanalysis, S.E. Vol. 23: 141–207.

Gibbard, Allan. "Morality as Consistency in Living: Korsgaard's Tanner Lectures." *Ethics* 110 (1999): 140–64.

Goffman, Erving. "Footing." In *Forms of Talk* (Philadelphia: University of Pennsylvania Press, 1981), 124–59.

The Presentation of Self in Everyday Life. New York: Anchor Books, 1959.

Halter, Marek. *Stories of Deliverance: Speaking with Men and Women who Rescued Jews from the Holocaust*, trans. Michael Bernard. Chicago: Open Court, 1998.

Hare, Caspar. "Voices from Another World: Must We Respect the Interests of People Who Do Not, and Will Never, Exist?" *Ethics* 117 (2007): 498–523.

Hempel, Carl G. "The Function of General Laws in History." In *Aspects of Scientific Explanation and Other Essays in the Philosophy of Science* (New York: The Free Press, 1965), 231–43.

Herman, Barbara. *Moral Literacy*. Cambridge, MA: Harvard University Press, 2007.

Johnston, Mark. "The Authority of Affect." *Philosophy and Phenomenological Research* 63 (2001): 181–214.

Joyce, James M. "Are Newcombe Problems Really Decisions?." *Synthese* 156 (2007): 537–62.

Kant, Immanuel. *The Groundwork of the Metaphysics of Morals*, trans. Mary Gregor. Cambridge: Cambridge University Press, 1997.

Kermode, Frank. *The Sense of an Ending: Studies in the Theory of Fiction*. New York: Oxford University Press, 2000.

Korsgaard, Christine. "Realism and Constructivism in Twentieth-Century Moral Philosophy." In *Philosophy in America at the Turn of the Century* (Charlottesville: Philosophy Documentation Center, 2003), 99–122.

Laird, J. D. "The Real Role of Facial Responses in Experience of Emotion: A Reply to Tourangeau and Ellsworth, and Others." *Journal of Personality and Social Psychology* **47** (1984): 909–17.

MacIntyre, Alasdair. "The Intelligibility of Action." In *Rationality, Relativism, and the Human Sciences*, ed. J. Margolis, M. Krausz, and R. M. Burian (Dordrecht: Martinus Nijhoff, 1986), 63–80.

Mackenzie, Catriona. "Bare Personhood? Velleman on Selfhood." *Philosophical Explorations* **10** (2007): 263–81.

Mackie, John. *Ethics: Inventing Right and Wrong.* Harmondsworth: Penguin Books, 1997.

McDowell, John. "Values and Secondary Qualities." In *Morality and Objectivity: A Tribute to J. L. Mackie*, ed. Ted Honderich (London: Routledge & Kegan Paul, 1985), 110–29.

McMahan, Jefferson. "Preventing the Existence of People with Disabilities." In *Quality of Life and Human Difference: Genetic Testing, Health Care, and Disability*, ed. David Wasserman, Jerome Bickenbach, and Robert Wachbroit (New York: Cambridge University Press, 2005), 142–71.

Mead, Andrew. "Bodily Hearing: Physiological Metaphors and Musical Understanding." *Journal of Music Theory* **43** (1999): 1–18.

Melden, A. I. *Free Action*. London: Routledge and Kegan Paul, 1961.

Mill, John Stuart. *On Liberty* New York: Barnes & Noble Books, 2004.

Morton, Adam. *The Importance of Being Understood: Folk Psychology as Ethics*. New York: Routledge, 2003.

Murdoch, Iris. *The Sovereignty of Good*. New York: Routledge and Kegan Paul, 1970.

"The Sublime and the Good." In *Existentialists and Mystics: Writings on Philosophy and Literature*, ed. Peter Conradi (New York: Penguin, 1997), 205–20.

Nagel, Thomas. "Concealment and Exposure." *Philosophy and Public Affairs* **27** (1998): 3–30; reprinted in *Concealment and Exposure* (New York: Oxford University Press, 2002), 3–26.

The Possibility of Altruism. Princeton, NJ: Princeton University Press, 1970.

Nussbaum, Martha. "Narrative Emotions: Beckett's Genealogy of Love." *Ethics* **98** (1988): 225–54.

Oliner, Pearl M. *Saving the Forsaken: Religious Culture and the Rescue of Jews in Nazi Europe.* New Haven, CT: Yale University Press, 2004.

Oliner, Samuel P., and Oliner, Pearl M. *The Altruistic Personality: Rescuers of Jews in Nazi Europe.* New York: The Free Press, 1988.

Parfit, Derek. *Reasons and Persons.* Oxford: Clarendon Press, 1984.

Pettit, Philip. "Substantive Moral Theory." *Social Philosophy and Policy* **25** (2008): 1–27.

Pinker, Steven. *The Language Instinct.* New York: William Morrow, 1994.

Plato. "Euthyphro," trans. G. M. A. Grube. In *Plato: Complete Works*, ed. John M. Cooper (Indianapolis: Hackett Publishing Company, 1997), 1–16.

Railton, Peter. "Alienation, Consequentialism, and the Demands of Morality." *Philosophy and Public Affairs* **13** (1984): 134–71.

"On the Hypothetical and Non-Hypothetical in Reasoning about Belief and Action." In *Ethics and Practical Reason*, ed. Garrett Cullity and Berys Gaut (Oxford: Clarendon Press, 1997), 53–79.

Raz, Joseph. *The Practice of Value*, ed. R. Jay Wallace. Oxford: Clarendon Press, 2003.

Sartre, Jean-Paul. *Being and Nothingness: An Essay on Phenomenological Ontology*, trans. Hazel E. Barnes. New York: Philosophical Library, 1956.

Sawyer, R. Keith. *Creating Conversations: Improvisation in Everyday Discourse.* Cresskill, NJ: Hampton Press, 2001.

Improvised Dialogues; Emergence and Creativity in Conversation. Westport, CT: Ablex Publishing, 2003.

Pretend Play as Improvisation: Conversation in the Preschool Classroom. Mahwah, NJ: Lawrence Erlbaum Associates, 1997.

Scanlon, Thomas M. *Moral Dimensions: Permissibility, Meaning, Blame.* Cambridge, MA: Harvard University Press, 2008.

What We Owe to Each Other. Cambridge, MA: Harvard University Press, 2000.

Schachter, S., & Singer, J. E. "Cognitive, Social and Physiological Determinants of Emotional State." *Psychological Review* **69** (1962): 379–99.

Schank, R. C., & Abelson, R. P. *Scripts, Plans, Goals, and Understanding: An Inquiry into Human Knowledge Structures.* Hillsdale, NJ: Lawrence Erlbaum Associates, 1977.

Schapiro, Tamar. "Compliance, Complicity, and the Nature of Nonideal Conditions." *Journal of Philosophy* **100** (2003): 329–55.

Shah, Nishi, and Velleman, J. David. "Doxastic Deliberation." *Philosophical Review* **114** (2005): 497–534.

Sherman, S. J. "On the Self-erasing Nature of Errors of Prediction." *Journal of Personality and Social Psychology* **39** (1980): 211–21.

Silverstein, Matthew. "Ethics as Practical." MS.

Snyder, Mark, & Klein, Olivier. "Construing and Constructing Others; On the Reality and the Generality of the Behavioral Confirmation Scenario." *Interaction Studies* **6** (2005): 53–67.

Strasberg, Lee. *A Dream of Passion: The Development of the Method.* New York: Plume, 1998.

Strawson, Galen. "Against Narrativity." *Ratio* **17** (2004): 428–52.

Strawson, P. F. "Freedom and Resentment." *Proceedings of the British Academy* **48** (1960): 1–25.

Street, Sharon. "Constructivism about Reasons." In *Oxford Studies in Metaethics* Vol. 3, ed. Russ Shafer-Landau (New York: Oxford University Press, 2008), 207–45.

Swann, William, Jr. *Resilient Identities: Self, Relationships, and the Construction of Social Reality.* New York: Basic Books, 1999.

"The Self and Identity Negotiation." *Interaction Studies* **6** (2005): 69–83.

Taylor, Charles. "Responsibility for Self." In *Free Will*, ed. Gary Watson (Oxford: Oxford University Press, 1982), 111–26.

"What Is Human Agency?" In *The Self*, ed. Theodore Mischel (Totowa, NJ: Rowman and Littlefield, 1977), 103–35.

Temkin, Larry. "Intransitivity and the Mere Addition Paradox." *Philosophy and Public Affairs* **16** (1987): 138–87.

Velleman, J. David. "Beyond Price." *Ethics* **118** (2008): 191–212.

"A Brief Introduction to Kantian Ethics." In *Self to Self*, 16–44.

"The Centered Self." In *Self to Self*, 253–83.

"Epistemic Freedom." *Pacific Philosophical Quarterly* **70** (1989): 73–97; reprinted in *The Possibility of Practical Reason*, 32–55.

"From Self-Psychology to Moral Philosophy." In *Self to Self*, 224–52.

"The Genesis of Shame." *Philosophy and Public Affairs* **30** (2001): 27–52; reprinted in *Self to Self*, 45–70.

"Identification and Identity," In *The Contours of Agency: Essays on Themes from Harry Frankfurt*, ed. Sarah Buss and Lee Overton (Cambridge, MA: MIT Press, 2001), 91–123; reprinted in *Self to Self*, 330–60.

"A Theory of Value." *Ethics.* **118** (2008): 410–36.

"Introduction." In *The Possibility of Practical Reason*, 1–31.

"Love as a Moral Emotion." *Ethics* **109** (1999): 338–74.

"Motivation by Ideal." *Philosophical Explorations* **5** (2002): 89–104; reprinted in *Self to Self*, 312–329.

"Narrative Explanation." *The Philosophical Review* **112** (2003): 1–25.

"On the Aim of Belief." In *The Possibility of Practical Reason*, 244–81.

"Persons in Prospect." *Philosophy and Public Affairs* **36** (2008): 222–88.

"The Possibility of Practical Reason." *Ethics* **106** (1996): 694–726; reprinted in *The Possibility of Practical Reason*, 170–99.

The Possibility of Practical Reason. Oxford: Oxford University Press, 2000.

Practical Reflection. Palo Alto, CA: CSLI Press, 2007.

"A Rational Super-Ego." *The Philosophical Review* **108** (1999): 529–58; reprinted in *Self to Self*: 129–55.

"The Self as Narrator." In *Autonomy and the Challenges to Liberalism: New Essays*, ed. Joel Anderson & John Christman (Cambridge: Cambridge University Press, 2005), 56–76; reprinted in *Self to Self*, 203–23.

Self to Self: Selected Essays. New York: Cambridge University Press, 2006.

"The Story of Rational Action". *Philosophical Topics* **21** (1993): 229–53; reprinted in *The Possibility of Practical Reason*, 144–69.

"The Voice of Conscience." *Proceedings of the Aristotelian Society* **99** (1999): 57–76; reprinted in *Self to Self*, 110–28.

"The Way of the Wanton." In *Practical Identity and Narrative Agency*, ed. Kim Atkins and Catriona MacKenzie (London: Routledge, 2007), 169–92.

"Well-Being and Time." *The Pacific Philosophical Quarterly* **72** (1991): 48–77; reprinted in *The Possibility of Practical Reason*, 56–84.

"What Good Is a Will?" In *Action in Context*, ed. Anton Leist (Berlin/New York: de Gruyter, 2007), 193–215.

"What Happens When Someone Acts?." *Mind* **101** (1992): 461–81; reprinted in The *Possibility of Practical Reason*, 123–43.

"Willing the Law." In *Practical Conflicts: New Philosophical Essays,* ed. Peter Baumann and Monika Betzler (Cambridge: Cambridge University Press, 2004), 27–56; reprinted in *Self to Self,* 284–311.

Walton, Kendall L. "Style and the Products and Processes of Art." In *The Concept of Style,* ed. Beryl Lang (Ithaca, NY: Cornell University Press, 1987), 72–103.

Wedgewood, Ralph. *The Nature of Normativity.* Oxford: Clarendon Press, 2007.

Williams, Bernard. "Consistency and Realism." *Proceedings of the Aristotelian Society* Supplementary Volume **40** (1966): 1–22.

"Ethics and the Fabric of the World." In *Making Sense of Humanity and Other Philosophical Papers* (Cambridge: Cambridge University Press, 1995), 172–81.

Ethics and the Limits of Philosophy. Cambridge, MA: Harvard University Press, 1985.

"Internal and External Reasons." In *Moral Luck* (Cambridge: Cambridge University Press, 1981), 101–13.

"Internal Reasons and the Obscurity of Blame." In *Making Sense of Humanity and Other Philosophical Papers* (Cambridge: Cambridge University Press, 1995), 35–45.

"Replies." In *World, Mind, and Ethics: Essays on the Ethical Philosophy of Bernard Williams,* ed. J. E. J. Altham and Ross Harrison (Cambridge: Cambridge University Press, 1995), 185–224.

Wittgenstein, Ludwig. *Philosophical Investigations,* trans. G. E. M. Anscombe Malden, MA: Blackwell Publishers, 2001.

Index

Abelson, Robert, 70, 194
acquaintance, 51
acting for a reason, 26, 36, 120
acting, improvisational, 12–16, 23,
    61, 62, 74, 76, 85–7, 89, 93, 94,
    98–100, 108, 110, 112, 129, 131,
    132, 150, 153, 162, 173–6, 185
acting, "method," 11–12, 28
action, 10, 29, 30, 36, 40, 129–34
    constitutive aim of, 64, 80, 81, 87,
        120, 127–9, 134–47, 149, 163
action-types, 5, 78, 79, 80
Adams, Robert Merrihew, 134
admiration, 41–5
akrasia. See weakness of will
ambivalence, 54, 55, 90
Anderson, Elizabeth A., 37, 201, 201
Anscombe, G.E.M., 71, 129, 131, 172
appropriateness. See correctness
aptness. See correctness
Arendt, Hannah, 203
Aristotle, 33, 185, 186, 190–1, 197,
    198
Aron, Arthur P., 38
Atkins, Kim, 10
attention, 18–25, 102, 103, 125, 196
attribution theory, 37–9
audience, 16, 18, 24, 62, 89, 93, 94,
    107, 132

authenticity, 69, 82, 102, 150, 151,
    159, 160, 162–4, 175, 177
autonomy, 79, 87, 94, 129–33, 137,
    143, 153, 169–72

bad faith, 25, 202
Baumann, Peter, 32, 214
belief, 29, 124, 125, 127, 133–4,
    141
belief, self-fulfilling, 106,
    130–3
Betzler, Monika , 32, 214
Bicchieri, Christina, 70
Bickenbach, Jerome, 49
Blackburn, Simon, 1
Block, Gay, 156
Boghossian, Paul, ix, xi, 140
Brakel, Linda, 100
Brodt, S.E, 38
Brooks, Peter, 193, 194, 197
Burian, R.M., 18
Buss, Sarah, 10, 89, 213

Carroll, Noël, 187–90, 191
Castañeda, Hector-Neri, 159
Categorical Imperative, 148, 161,
    165, 168–72, 176
causal explanation, xi, 4, 13, 16, 27,
    163, 185–9, 201, 203, 205

Cavell, Stanley, 103
commitments, 104–8, 109, 116, 180, 202
common knowledge, xi, 65, 166–78, 184
conflict, interpersonal, 67, 86, 150, 152, 173, 182
conflict, psychological, 32, 84, 90, 150
conflict of values, 56
conscience, 88–114, 151, 161, 161
consequentialism, 178–84
consistency, 38, 48–58
Copp, David, xi
correctness, 27, 35–7, 40, 42, 57, 122–9, 134–47, 162–4, 204
Cullity, Garrett, 124

Dancy, Jonathan, 121
D'Arms, Justin, 45
Darwall, Stephen L., xi, 141, 208
Davidson, Donald, 72
dead ends, 33, 163
deception, 4–6, 12, 17, 25, 61, 64, 84, 86, 89, 102, 150, 151, 157
decision theory, 19, 59
DeLancy, Craig, 196
de Sousa, Ronald, 194, 196
diplomacy, 69
disgust, 44
Dreier, James, 147
Drucker, Malka, 156
Duclos, S.E., 39
Dutton, Donald G, 38

efficiency, 27
Egan, Andy, xi
embarrassment, 95
emotion, xi, 12, 26, 51, 94–104, 180, 190, 191–2, 195–200, 202
Enoch, David, xi, 115, 142, 204, 208
Erdur, Melis, xi, 115
Evans, Matthew, 134
evolution, 30
Eythyphro argument, 134

Ferrero, Luca, 142
feud, 47
fiction, 12, 13, 14, 174
folk psychology, 13, 21, 27, 60
Forster, E.M., 187, 192
Fraisse, Paul, 193
Frankfurt, Harry, 10, 89, 108, 167, 213
Freud, Sigmund, 100–1, 104, 109, 111, 193

Gaut, Berys, 124
generality, 45–8, 63, 81, 150, 151, 152, 161
Gibbard, Allan, 56, 147, 148
Goffman, Erving, 12, 17, 67, 70, 76, 78
good, 27, 114, 139, 179, 180
guided responses, 35
guilt, xi, 94, 98–100, 109, 111, 112, 151, 158

habituation, 92, 160
Hanser, Matthew, 55
Hare, Caspar , 48, 209
Hatzimoysis, Anthony, 98
Hempel, Carl G., 189
Herman, Barbara, 1, 40, 154
holism, 19, 42, 44, 57, 159
Holocaust, 155
human nature, 1, 16, 44, 45, 136, 151, 154, 160, 162, 180
Hume, David, 101, 118
humor, 35, 43, 45, 192
Hussain, Nadeem, 115

idealizations, 164–5, 176–84
identity negotiation, 66–8
imperatives, 116
improvisational acting. *See* acting, improvisational
inauthenticity, 17, 26, 61, 90–2, 94, 99, 161, 180
'in character', 38

inconsistency. *See* consistency
inescapability, 16, 115, 116, 136, 137,
140, 143, 167, 170
intelligibility, 13, 18, 27, 31, 40, 81,
136, 139, 165, 177, 185, 199
intentions for the future. *See*
commitments
introspection, 23

Jacobson, Daniel, 45
Johnston, Mark, 22, 40
Joyce, James M., 130
justification, 122–8, 136, 138, 204
circular, 138, 140–2, 146

Kant, Immanuel, xi, 2, 31, 59, 80,
110, 115, 116, 148, 155,
165–72
"Kantian strategy," 125, 143, 147,
148, 150, 213
Kennett, Jeannette, x
Kermode, Frank, 192, 195
Kingdom of Ends, 176, 182, 184
Klein, Oliver, 67
Korsgaard, Christine, ix, 16, 148
Krausz, M., 18, 79, 210

Laird, J.D., 39
Leist, Anton, 24, 138
love, xi, 51–8, 101–4, 199
lying. *See* deception

MacIntyre, Alasdair, 18, 79
Mackenzie, Catriona, x, 10, 213
Mackie, John, 116, 117
making sense, 13–17, 21–2, 28, 30,
32, 39, 40, 42–8, 60, 65, 75, 80,
91, 108, 132, 146, 156, 159, 163,
173, 182, 186
Margolis, J., 18, 79, 210
Martin, Adrienne, ix
Matthews, Steve, x
McDowell, John, 3, 40, 149
McMahan, Jefferson, 49, 53
Mead, Andrew, 195

meaning, 204–6
Melden, A.I., 71
metaethics, 2–4, 6, 157, 165
method acting. *See* acting, "method"
Mill, John Stuart, 83
Miller, Christian, ix
mode of presentation, 51–8
moral discourse, 151–4, 157, 173
moral relativism, 162–4
moral responsibility. *See*
responsibility
moral theory, 6, 161–84
morality, 1–6, 48, 85–7, 99, 104, 107,
109, 112, 114, 115–17, 147–58,
161–84
Morton, Adam, 64, 65

Nagel, Thomas, 69, 95, 146
narrative, xi, 4, 7, 163, 204–6
normativity, 6, 13, 16, 27, 31, 40, 75
realism about, 115, 116, 139
Nussbaum, Martha, 199

objectivity, 40–6, 80, 87, 114,
115–29, 134–47, 162–4, 165–70
"openness of the future," 136, 148
Overton, Lee, 10, 89, 213

Parfit, Derek, 51, 53
Pauer-Studer, Herlinde, xi
personhood, 113
Pettit, Philip, 149, 149
Piller, Christian, ix
Pinker, Steven, 195
Plato, 89, 134
Plunkett, David, xi, 115
Possibility of Practical Reason The, i, xi,
10, 19, 68, 107, 118, 127, 130,
179, 201, 212, 213, 214
practical identity, 16
Practical Reflection, i, xi, 213
practices, 5, 45, 79, 80, 154, 180
Principle of Utility, 161, 178
prisoner's dilemma, 4, 47
privacy, 98

procrastination, 32
procreation, 48–58
punishment, 111–13

Railton, Peter, 124, 142, 181
Raz, Joseph, 1, 211
realism. *See* normativity, realism
    about; values, realism about
reasoning, instrumental, 30, 64, 77,
    87, 146, 179, 201, 202
reasoning, practical, x, 1–3, 4–6, 7,
    18–33, 79, 114, 117–47, 150,
    165, 186
  as experimental, 85, 111, 114, 149,
    161, 162–4
  divisions in, 33, 83, 93–4, 104,
    114, 163, 204–6
reasoning, theoretical, 17, 29, 31,
    136, 140
reasons, 2, 18, 118, 144
  as "counting in favor," 19, 121
  for acting, 19, 22, 31, 36, 146,
    166–72
  for believing, 124
  for valuing, 36, 40
  wrong kind, 45
relativism. *See* moral relativism
resoluteness. *See* commitments
respect, 86, 113
responsibility, 112–14
roles, 25, 66, 68, 69, 81, 82, 84–7,
    93, 94, 102, 103, 110, 150, 153,
    162–4
Rosenkoetter, Timothy, 166

Sartre, Jean-Paul, 25, 202
Sawyer, R. Keith, 12, 70, 174
Scanlon, Thomas M., 98, 121
scenarios, 70–6, 78, 81–3, 87, 150,
    151–4, 157, 162–4, 173, 175–6
Schank, Roger, 70, 194
Schapiro, Tamar, 1
"shmagency," 146, 149, 213

Schneider, M., 39
Schroeder, Mark, ix
science, 3, 111, 149, 154, 161, 164
Sebo, Jeff, xi
Self to Self, i, x, xi, 10, 17, 33, 38, 51,
    69, 89, 95, 98, 100, 101, 160,
    165, 212, 213
self-awareness, 17, 19, 21, 24, 26, 31,
    32, 136
self-deception, 61, 64, 90, 94, 102,
    105, 131, 203
self-enactment, 14–18, 25, 59–61,
    64, 85–7, 89, 93, 96, 102, 103,
    108, 129, 184
self-fulfilling belief. *See* belief,
    self-fulfilling
self-interest, 4, 54, 68
self-reform, 32, 83
self-trust. *See* commitments
self-understanding, drive toward,
    15, 17, 26, 27, 28, 38, 61, 64, 66,
    133, 136
self-understanding, shared, 61–6,
    69, 77, 80, 86, 112, 150, 153,
    160, 173–8, 184
Setiya, Kieran, 115
Shafer-Landau, 126, 142, 209, 212
Sexter, L., 39
Shah, Nishi, xi, 29, 115, 134, 212
shame, xi, 94–8, 109, 112, 151, 158
Sherman, S.J., 92
Sie, Maureen, ix
Silverstein, Matthew, xi, 115, 121, 212
simplicity, 62–6, 81–2, 162, 165
Smith, Matthew Noah, ix
Smith, Michael, ix
Snyder, Mark, 67
social disqualification, 95, 98, 109, 111
state of nature, 6
Steele, John, 195
Strachey, James, 100
Strasberg, Lee, 11, 12
Strawson, Galen, 204

Strawson, Peter, 113
Street, Sharon, xi, 115, 126, 139, 145
superego, 100–1, 104, 109
Swann, William, 66–8

Taylor, Charles, 103
Temkin, Larry, 48, 212
Toh, Kevin, 110
truth, 116, 125, 127, 133–4, 141
truth-telling. *See* deception

understanding as comprehension, 62–4, 81, 82, 163, 164, 185
universality. *See* generality
unthinkable. *See* volitional necessity
Utilitarianism, 178, 180–4

value, 37, 41–8, 181
    realism about, 46, 51, 56–8, 150, 160, 181
value judgment, 35

values, 81, 110, 162–4, 173
    shared, 47, 82, 150, 151, 154, 160, 180
valuing, 36–7, 40, 159
Van Lighten, O., 39
Velleman, Shelley, 195
volitional necessity, 108–9, 110, 151

Wachbroit, Robert, 49
Walton, Kendall L., 195
Wasserman, David, 49
way of life, 76, 79, 160, 161, 162, 180
weakness of will, 15
Wedgwood, Ralph, 127
White, Morton, 187
Williams, Bernard, 2, 20–2, 48, 115–20, 145, 147, 148, 214
wishful thinking, 91, 93
Wittgenstein, Ludwig, 71, 79, 80
Wolff, Jonathan, x
Wright, Helena, xi

Zimbardo, P.G., 38